Journey on the Outside
My Life as an Activist

Mark M. Moore

The Ridge Enterprise Group
Copyright 2021
Paperback ISBN: 978-1-7332778-1-5

Dedication

To my wife Melissa. Encouraging me to write this book was among the least things she has done to turn my existence into a life.

Contents

A Different Sort of Journey 1

The New Me 15

The Man from Thunder Mountain 31

An Officer and a Gentleman 45

Educator 57

Registered Republican 73

All Kinds of Changes 101

The Campaign for Lt. Governor and Moving On 127

Life and Politics 145

The End of the World as We Know it 157

The Illusion of Freedom 181

I Sue the State 195

ACCESS 219

Other Books by Mark Moore 223

Chapter One

A Different Sort of Journey

I have a theory that we are all born who we are, and we spend our lifetime becoming ourselves. Or at least some version of ourselves. A twist in this idea is that we can hit a fork in the road and become either a better or a worse version of who we were meant to be. For example, consider the great boxer George Foreman, who won held the Heavyweight Boxing Championship briefly as a young man, and then again when he was well into his forties. The menacing tower of hostility that was the young George Foreman became the jovial and affable older George Foreman. But even in that process, I am convinced that the man just became a better version of himself, not someone different.

Both versions for example, were world champion boxers. The people that knew him best would probably tell you that he became a new man, but he became a new George Foreman. Not someone else. The vices of the old man were somehow transformed into virtues in the new one.

I know that's a weird place to start a book about my political and personal journey. But if I was conventional then I don't think I'd have anything of value to write to you. I too had to become a better version of myself. A journey has a beginning where things are a certain way, and then things change. Not just the scenery, but the traveler. If the story is a happy one then at the end the traveler becomes who they were meant to be, perhaps in a place that is better for them than even they intended. If the tale is a sad one, their journey ends with them becoming some other version of themselves. I have seen plenty of both. Maybe if I tell you where I started out, and some of the forks in the road I faced, and the lessons I learned from it, it will help you in your journey.

I was born in Houston, Texas in 1961 in the aftermath of hurricane Camille. But there were other storms coming too. The world was about to change. It was hard to say what change was the biggest, but the pattern of the times was that existing authorities of all stripes were being challenged. My home was no exception.

When I was nine years old my father called my sister and I into the living room and told us, with tears in his eyes, that he and our mother were getting a divorce. I really can't remember much of my childhood before that moment. What I know is mostly from what others have told me or prompted me on. I do vaguely remember getting kicked out of my preschool, called "The Little Red Schoolhouse" in the now-defunct Westbury Square. The teacher was shaking her finger in my face and fussing at me, and I bit her finger. This wasn't the only authority figure I defied. According to my mother, in Sunday School I would just get up and leave and find my parents. The befuddled teachers were left sputtering.

Now you might read that and think "Mark was a terrible child". But the truth is I was hyper-compliant to my parents. I was the "good kid" and my little sister was the hellion, to the extent there was one. Mother told me that on the rare occasions when I did something wrong, I would immediately admit my guilt and say that I deserved whatever punishment was meted out. My sister would run and fight rather than submit to a spanking. Thinking back to my five-year-old self as best I can, and comparing it to my nature, I must have concluded that my parents had earned the right to boss and discipline me. They had proven their good intentions. These other grown-ups? Who the hell did they think they were? Even then, it wasn't that I was against authority. I was against illegitimate authority!

When I was five it was time to send me off to public school, because that's what everyone did back then. No one questioned that the proper thing to do was to send your child to the government schools. Given my history, my mother was terrified of what I would do when thrown into that environment. She tells me that before the first day of school she explained to me that the teachers were standing in for her, that they were basically operating under the authority of the parents. Therefore, I should listen to them just like I did my parents. The light went on. The way she told me the story, I said "Oh, ok" and was a model student for years, right up until the divorce.

Ironically, and almost certainly unknown to her, the legal theory under which public schools operated was changing at that time. In the past, schools were viewed as operating "in loco parentis", that is, for the parent. But the legal doctrine had been changing, and teachers and schools were from that time forward legally acting as agents of the state, not the parents. But that's probably for another book.

Speaking of books, the thing I do remember about my childhood that went right was that my parents signed me up for every "Time-Life Encyclopedia" series they could find. The seller would mail them to the house, either one or a few at a time. I would devour them. It didn't matter if it was about any branch of science or history. I craved knowledge.

At the time, I probably thought my mother bore more responsibility for the end of their marriage than my father. I went to live with him, and my sister went to live with my mother. In truth, my mom just was too much of a lady to burden me with her side of the story. I found out as an adult that he did plenty to precipitate it. However, I didn't know that as a youth or a young man, and this probably contributed to trust issues with the opposite sex. When I hit puberty, I was attracted to them, but I did not relate to or understand them. As painful as that was, it kept me from making some bad mistakes later in life and I will just go ahead and spoil it for you by saying that after a very long time I found someone I could trust and this part of my life had a happy ending.

So, there I was, being raised by my father with basically no mother or siblings in the house. He was my sole parental figure from age ten to fifteen. My father was an amazing man. He married my mother, who was "Miss Houston Universe" and about eleven years his junior. Not many years after the divorce, he would marry the woman who would become my stepmother, who was Miss Galveston and a whopping 24 years younger than him. She still has the magic. Her name is now Essie Hetrick and she is the reigning Ms. Senior USA. He had a way with the ladies, to put it mildly. He had a way with a lot of people. Essie once said that he could be equally at ease at a black-tie dinner with dignitaries or eating tacos with first-generation Mexicans on the front porch. He was extremely witty and could connect to almost anybody.

That made him a fantastic salesman, and he also had a knack for making money. When I was younger, before the divorce, I remember that our garage was always stocked with all kinds of interesting light bulbs. That was because he was a sales representative for Sylvania Light Bulb Company and he had lots of samples. They were taking on G.E. which was dominant on store shelves. So, he had that big strike against him, but as one person said, "He walked into a room like he owned it." Despite the limitations of his body (he was a juvenile diabetic and was told that he would not live to see forty but with discipline lasted until age fifty-four) his spirit was indomitable.

He was always thinking of ways to sell. He noticed that a big gas-station chain was giving something away "free with fill up". He found the manager and told the guy "the product you are giving away lasts years. You want something they need lots of and must keep coming back for. That's either toilet paper or light bulbs. You don't want to give away toilet paper, do you?" It worked, and they distributed to a national chain, though they took the sale away from dad because it was over multiple territories.

Despite that, he was the number two salesman in the nation for them. And the number one guy was not cut out for management. When the time came to pick a new manager, dad figured on getting the job. They picked someone else. At a company party, he pigeon-holed the big boss and asked him "why"? The guy looked at my father and then pointed to the bar lined with his colleagues. "You see those guys over there, Max? I can walk up to anyone of 'em and tell you what they are going to say next. No one knows what you are going to say next."

He didn't feel chastised by this experience. He didn't take it as a sign that he should start thinking and speaking more convention-ally. Instead, he figured that they did not want or deserve a man with his particular talents. He quit the company and went into real estate, where he found tremendous success.

He was just starting out in real estate when the divorce came. He would work Houston on Monday through early Friday and then he and I would head to Galveston. There he would sell beach lots all day, and then we would fish from a pier by night. I was walking the beach alone most of the day, but I was not the most social person around, so I didn't even know I was lonely.

It was mostly the same back in Houston. In fact, I remember this one poor kid from across the street, he wanted to be my friend. I wanted to be by myself. I physically threw him out of the house. I liked being alone with my thoughts, reading books, or putting together a vast array of models of World War Two military equipment. I was an anti-social nerd.

I was also chunky. When I was an infant, my mom thought I was allergic to the formula, so she kept switching me to different stuff. She wound up using "Eagle Brand Condensed Milk" which was loaded with sugar and fat. My dad's friend Morton, who was a rough teaser, said I looked like a "living Buddha" as an infant. I was still pretty hefty in fourth and fifth grade.

Some of the kids used to tease me about it, and other stuff. I did not take kindly to it, but I was still in hyper-compliant mode to school authorities. This started to change. The teacher that year was a gentle young black man that looking back I did not treat fairly. I thought he should have maintained better order and discipline in the classroom, like for example confronting the main guy who was provoking me. The kid was calling me dirty names most days of the week. My dad was old school. He told me the next time that guy calls you a dirty name, hit him in the face.

I am ashamed to write to you that I did just that. I was waiting for the chance to do that, and I did it right in the class and right in front of the teacher. The kid started sobbing. I was such a little Pharisee in my heart that I was OK with it. Today of course any student doing that would be in real trouble. That teacher just had me write one-hundred sentences. A few years later, when I had grown past this young man in every possible way, I realized that the kid was just a pathetic figure. He had what we today would recognize as learning disabilities, and he wanted to make fun of a good student who was wound up too tight, and I fit the bill.

There was another kid that was also taunting me. I grabbed him and poked him in the eye. One of the onlookers there thought I didn't do much to the kid and said he would have done worse, but his father had to take him in for an eye exam. The truth was, while I started the year a "fat kid" by the end of it I was starting to hit puberty. I saw myself as the victim, but in reality, I was larger and stronger than my classmates.

Well, there is such a thing as "blowback" and the kid I hit in the face was friends with a rough kid in the school who I will call "Lee". One who by age twelve had stolen motorcycles. He also had a reputation as one of the toughest kids in the school. Lee put the word out that he wanted to fight me on a certain day. Some people were glad to let me know that too. I was too stupid and full of anger to be afraid.

But before the showdown I came upon a group with a friend of his in it. The leader of this little group, older and from the Junior High School I think, suggested we fight in what I took to be a sporting sort of way. He didn't have to ask me twice, that's how tightly wound I was. I started landing some punches and his buddies teased him about getting whipped. He decided to quit boxing and go for the wrestle, getting me in a headlock. One of the others, ostensibly his friend, hollered out that his nuts were open, and I could hit him there. When I answered that this was just for fun and I wasn't going to do that in a fight like this, he let me go and I could tell there was some respect there. But he also claimed that Lee beat him fighting on a regular basis. Unphased, I said we were about to find out if he can beat me. I now wonder if the whole thing wasn't a "set up" designed to psych me out.

It seemed like the whole elementary school was there on the playground on the day the fight was supposed to occur. Where the adults were, I had no idea, and didn't even think about it at the time. The guy said he wanted to fight me, so I was there to fight. I had no one at my back. He had a dozen hangers-on and I'd say the rest of the hundred-plus present were just there to see some violence. But a funny thing happened. As I walked across the field toward Lee, he started walking backward. I walked forward some more, and he walked backward some more. Finally, he left the field.

I am ashamed to tell you that not many days later I was provoked by a guy named Kurt to go to Lee's house and ask him "if he wanted to play". He asked if I was going to ask him to fight. I said I was. He demurred. Kurt was urging us on, but after a couple of questions I left. Sometime later, someone got ahold of his diary and told me about the entry for our initial encounter. He had written that he was supposed to fight someone but "the guy is big and I kind of like him." For the first time, I got outside of my own self-righteousness to wonder "was I a jerk"? The answer was "yes" but I wasn't quite there yet. I heard as an adult that "Lee" wound up a very tough customer and spent time in prison. Looking back, if it's true it was only by the grace of God that it wasn't me. Not stealing motorcycles, but between having a poor temper and a propensity to resort to violence it could have been something worse.

I had never considered myself an athlete, I was frequently picked last on the playground. But I was still growing and with my newly discovered "talent" I was about to move to another phase of my life. By August before my sixth-grade year I was physically way ahead of my peers at five-foot nine inches. My father, eying my pudginess, had fed me steak and spinach all year long before anyone had ever heard of the Keto Diet. It worked. I was a lean one-hundred and twenty-four pounds. My father asked me if I wanted to sign up for pee-wee league football. I did. Badly. I still wanted to be a compliant student and make my dad proud. But I also realized that I relished "battle". I was probably awash in testosterone for the first time in my life and had no idea how to handle it.

It turned out that there was a weight limit for the league- at the date they signed up, players had to weigh under one-hundred and twenty pounds. It was probably to keep kids who developed early, like me, from hurting normal kids. Of course, when I went to sign up, I was five pounds over the limit. But sign up wasn't over for three more days. I skipped eating for three days straight and went back for the last weigh-in. I was 119 pounds. Some of the other kids on the team had been playing organized football for three years. I had hardly played any sandlot football, but I craved contact and was highly disruptive on both sides of the line. Our team wasn't very good, but I found a much-needed acceptable outlet for my hostilities.

My sixth-grade year I had teachers that I respected more, including a black man named Mr. Graves. He ran the school-guard crossing program. There were about fifteen students who worked flags that stopped traffic and let the younger kids cross the street safely. They had vests and shoulder belts and everything. To my shock, Mr. Graves asked me if I wanted to be second-in-command of the program, going around checking to make sure everyone was present and on task. I guess they figured, wisely, that I was the kind of person who could either be an "outlaw" or a "cop". To save me from myself, they made me a cop.

Thankfully, even if I didn't always want to hang around people, I did want to protect the younger and weaker students. It turned out that even if I wasn't sociable, I was a protector, not a predator. There was a way the authorities could turn my strengths to good account, and they were wise enough to do that. I was devoted to the job, and loved my teachers, especially Mr. Graves. No one was teasing me. I was part of a team both with the crossing guard program and the Pee-Wee football team. I would not call myself a people-person, but I was less anti-social.

Junior high was a bit of a restart, like it is for everyone. It was probably less painful for me because the biggest angst kids have at that age is being "popular". I was almost like that meme of the character Ron Swanson that says "Friends......one to three is sufficient". I wasn't good with girls, but it didn't bother me much. Truth is, I wasn't that into them. So long as I got to play football and run track, and maybe use my pellet gun to shoot rats with my buddy Clyde once in a while, life was good. The rest of my time was spent alone, thinking and building models of military equipment from World War Two. I hung out with my dad.

One thing that was different for me is that I was exposed to a large number of classmates who were African-American. They used to bus them in from across town. The suburban Dixiecrats who lived in my neighborhood named all the schools around there after Confederate symbols. My school was "Albert Sidney Johnston Jr. High." He was a confederate general. But nobody got the hint, I counted fourteen busloads of black kids coming to that gigantic school every day. The school was so huge that it was still majority white and Hispanic, but there was a sizable contingent of kids of African ancestry.

There was no weight-limit in that league. I wasn't small at 5'-11" and around 170 pounds, but I wasn't the biggest either. Especially when I was one of four eighth graders moved to play on the ninth-grade team. That was the year my father saw that I wasn't just bigger and stronger than everyone else, somehow, the pudgy nerd had turned into an athlete. The four who moved up to the ninth-grade team were me, another white guy who had failed twice and was two years older than the rest of us, and two black guys named Ivory and Jesse. This continued in track season, where I put the shot, ran the 440-yard dash, and anchored the mile relay team. I wasn't great in track, but I was good enough that when only eight uniforms came in and the coaches decided to hand them out to their "top eight", I got one. I was the only white kid who did.

Now you might think given my past that there would be friction throwing me in a new situation and a diverse group like that. You might think I would not get along with my black team-mates or fellow students. But the truth was the exact opposite. Maybe it was a little of my father's gifts coming out, or more likely that I felt like an alien in my own culture, so their different culture was no obstacle at all for me. It was just something new to learn, and I had an inquisitive mind. Being around black people didn't get me out of my comfort zone at all, because I had no comfort zone off the football field or track. So, there was no problem with comfort, or for that matter with fear. Some kids might be afraid of being thrown into such a milieu, but as you might deduce from reading to this point, it never occurred to me to be afraid of anything except failing. It wasn't even that I was brave. Courageous people overcome their fears. It never occurred to me to be afraid. It was just more people who were different from me, like about everyone else.

Despite that, I would describe myself as slightly anti-social at this point. When I was in eighth grade the coaches moved four of us up to the ninth-grade team. The older players expected me to defer to them. That wasn't going to happen, and as usual I didn't get along with everyone. But it wasn't a racial thing, the guys from my neighborhood were worse about it. Eventually, I'd say I earned the respect of most of them. I was the only guy on the offensive line to start every game and got second-team all-district. Life was tolerable, even if I saw the "sock-hops" and music and culture of the day and felt even then that "this is off, something is wrong here."

My dad made a bit of an effort to go to church. He decided he would "let me choose" where we would go, hoping I suppose that I would "own" the choice. He took me to a Church of Christ, where there was no instrumental music and the focus was on content. Then he took me to the local Baptist church, where they put on a much more emotion-oriented show. I said I liked the Church of Christ better. That was the wrong answer. He was a Baptist who was a theology major at Baylor before flunking out because "the other people in my Zoology class were pre-Med".

We wound up not going much anyway, but something started happening where I wound up getting on my bicycle and peddling over to an Assembly of God Church, ironically, more like the Baptist church in that respect. Still, I was a little Pharisee. I thought I was the "good guy" and of course my enemies were "bad guys" who, if I ever decided to "smite them", surely had it coming.

I had not had any contact with my mother or my sister during this time. It was an ugly divorce. But the court order really gave her custody. Eventually the lawyers were called in to sort it out. I went to a meeting where my dad waited outside while my mom's lawyer and my dad's lawyer talked to me. I had my own "list of conditions" for visitation that, thinking back, were ridiculous. It was almost like we were doing a hostage exchange, that's how little trust I had. My mom's lawyer kept pressing me. He said that my sister had made no demands and had agreed to everything.

I asked the lawyer if she really agreed to everything with no objections. He reiterated that she did. I looked at him and said "If she is willing to compromise, why should I? Let's do it my way." This was a kid in eighth grade saying this. My dad's lawyer chimed in "he's got you there." Embarrassed, mom's lawyer went off-script (mom would never have authorized this) and threatened to have me removed by law from my father's house and placed in a juvenile facility until I was eighteen. I instantly replied that when I got out, I would know who to come looking for. He asked if I was threatening him and I told him he was threatening me. I wasn't having it. My dad's lawyer stepped in and defused the situation. Afterward he told my dad, "Your son comes on like a two-ton garlic truck." As you can tell, I was still way too intense and not what you would call an easy-going or pleasant person. Fortunately, we got the visits worked out.

I started visiting my mom and my sister again, and my sister visited Dad and me. Dad got us horses. Dad had really moved up in the world and ran the sales offices of the "Development" part of "Mitchell Energy and Development". Pirates Beach and Cove was just one of the offices. Now it is practically a metropolis, but I remember when it was just a few houses and his team was selling lots there and other places.

You can tell I think a lot of my dad. I was with him through high and low back then. My first political experience was with him volunteering for a campaign for some Republican politician. He must have been more involved than I thought. When he died the Texas State Legislature passed a resolution honoring his life. I still have it someplace.

I remember asking him why he didn't run for office. It was one of the few times I saw him choke up. His usual air of confidence was gone. With a tear running down his cheek, he cited his personal failings. He said a man who couldn't hold his own family together did not deserve to be elected. That if someone can't manage their own life well, then they shouldn't aspire to run the government. Of course, I protested that he was a better man than any of them. But I didn't mention politics again either. If only he could see what goes on now. People who can't even run their own lives want to run ours! We have a system that almost prefers flawed people, maybe because they are easier to control if you have something on them. But I digress, other than giving you an idea where my standards are.

Chapter Two

The New Me

Some of you reading this book may think I am a jerk. Others of you who have a more charitable outlook may be wondering "when did you *stop* being such a jerk?" Well, the bottom line is not any different from a man I mentioned at the start of this book – George Foreman. God saved me. Some of you may not accept that as a valid answer, but that's my answer. It's ok to put it on the back shelf a while as you read on. I can't do justice to describing my political journey without describing at least some of my spiritual journey.

I had no idea what salvation was. I was a clueless thirteen-year-old trying to be righteous by good works. And like most who practice righteousness by their own good works, I was far off from the proper path. If you are no good at it, you feel hopeless and give up. If you can convince yourself that your sins are not so bad as those of the other guys, then you get self-righteous and unforgiving. That was me. That is the natural tendency I must look out for.

Dad had gravitated to something called "The World-Wide Church of God" led by a fellow named Herbert W. Armstrong. Not that they had a local church, he was a radio preacher. But they had a free monthly magazine called "The Plain Truth". It was mostly focused on "end-times" stuff, but one of its recurring themes was that mainstream Christianity had things wrong, because they were not looking to the scriptures. Month after month, these magazines would describe a church doctrine, or practice, and then cite scriptures which appeared to conflict with them. Their point was that the scriptures should be the authority for church practice, but even the ones that claimed that they were abiding by the scriture didn't follow it. Believers, they said, should follow scripture alone and not decide what they believe on any other basis.

I decided to take their advice. I threw out all commentaries on scripture, including their magazine, and just started reading the bible. Not that I was a Christian at that time. I didn't even understand what Christianity was.

I talked to mom and told her what I was doing. I also said that looking at what scripture asks us to do, I just could not meet the requirements of a Christian. She told me to read the book of Romans. The first eight chapters at least. I remember sitting there at the desk in my room. I had a nice big white desk, with a red adjustable lamp. It was perfect for putting together scale models of Hitler's tanks. But now I was using it for bible study. I opened up the Bible to Romans and started reading those first eight chapters.

What I was doing, though I didn't know the name theologians had given it, was going down "the Roman Road". It laid out God's plan of salvation quite clearly. It started with the idea that all were under sin, and that we could not pull ourselves up by our own spiritual bootstraps. But the real purpose of the Law of Moses wasn't really to give us a way to earn our own right standing with a holy God. It was to teach us that we couldn't get there on our own. It was meant to show us how short of righteousness we were. There would be no way we could dare to take a hard, honest look at our own condition except for one thing- Jesus fulfilled the Law for us.

So, it wasn't about how good you could be, rather it was about how good God can be. We had to learn to trust Him, not ourselves or even the Law. If our faith is real, good works will eventually follow, but it won't be a struggle, it will just be a consequence of who we now are in Christ. I don't have the words to say it like Paul said it, but that was the gist.

I thought back to my efforts to be good. Not just my sins, but even my righteousness was flawed. If anything, my religion was closer to the Pharisees who opposed Jesus than the religion of Jesus. By the grace of God, I somehow saw that I could not earn my way into heaven by works. I couldn't get into a favorable bargaining position with God. But that was OK, I could at last face the truth about myself and my condition because of what Christ did, and what it demonstrated about God's nature. He wasn't looking to step on us as soon as we messed up. He was looking to forgive. And if someday we were made into people able to live eternally in a realm where every desire in our heart could be fulfilled at once, then it would have to be His doing in us, not our own efforts.

That's when I bowed my head and prayed what I would later understand was called "the sinner's prayer" in religious circles. I asked God to forgive me, and wash me clean, and make me right His way. I accepted His Son as both "Savior", and "Lord". And I accepted God as Father. A father so representative of everything that a father was supposed to be, that even my earthly father was at best a pale shadow of the reality that was God. That is what I understood that night.

When I woke up the next morning, I was the same person, with the same flaws, but I believe I was also a new person. A better version of me came alive. Tiny at first, but growing. Maybe you can get a hint of it as you read on.

My mother and her new husband moved to Arkansas sometime during all this. That left a hole for me, because I was re-bonding with her, and with my sister. She had married someone who had been in the neighborhood and who had two children that I was already friends with growing up, before they moved off to Conroe. I had started visiting them there, but the extreme Northwest Corner of Arkansas was a long way from the flatlands of Houston. This was a shame because hanging out with them was good for me.

Ninth grade football season came, and I had an even better season - starting both ways and making first team all-district. The same four of us that were moved up the year before were team captains. I became President of the Fellowship of Christian Athletes huddle. I won't say that was the end of my fighting, but even that got better. My two or three best buddies did not share my lunch period, but I made my move to the "Cool Kids" table. Actual cheerleaders were speaking to me! I wouldn't say I fit in, but if the party was big enough, I got invited. I hated almost every minute of the couple I actually attended.

I had a new stepmother too. Essie, or YaYa as we called her back then, had married my dad. It was a ceremony that took place at my grandparents' house on the lake. He had teased her that she was committing to "love honor and obey" him. She then secretly went to the minister and directed him to change her vows to the vaguer "love, honor, and cherish". Dad barely avoided cracking up laughing in the middle of the ceremony when the preacher said the line. He immediately deduced what had happened.

She was an assertive person no doubt, but she was not at all responsible for the plot twist that happens next. We got along fine. She was not that much older than me and it was good for me to have a woman in the house so I could have some exposure to and figure out something about the other half of the earth's population. My dad passed on almost forty years ago, and Essie and I are still friends, and indeed family.

That Christmas Vacation, we called it that back then, I went to Northwest Arkansas for the first time to see my mom and stepfather. They had a big house on almost forty acres atop "Thunder

Mountain". It was a whole new, and enchanting, world for me. I remember when I saw the shadow of a cloud on the side of a mountain for the first time. I'd never seen that before, since Houston was so flat. Everything on that trip just seemed so right. I connected deeply with every soul under that roof, not just my mother and sister. It almost seemed like I had been born in the wrong place, that the hills of Arkansas were where I was meant to be. The Spirit moved me. Literally.

I went back to Texas when Christmas break was over, but something was wrong. I never knew how unhappy I had been until that time. I would start crying, for no reason. This didn't happen once, but numerous times. This was in spite of the fact that everything about my life in Houston was better than it had been before. I had no idea what was going on, just that I had to get back to Arkansas and the people there, even if it meant leaving my father and the life I had known and starting over. A new life. After all, wasn't that what I asked for when I prayed at my desk?

I called my mom and asked her to come get me. We didn't tell my father. I guess I left him a note. They just showed up at school and picked me up and drove me to rural Northwest Arkansas. I would not see my father again for three years. I ran away from home so to speak. I hated to do it to him, but the desire to go was overwhelming. It was beyond logic, or reason, or anything else you might have gathered that I am. I was grateful that he had an attractive new wife to console him.

And that last point brings me to what may be the oddest part of this tale yet. Years later, I was visiting with Essie when she told me this story. She said that shortly after I ran away from home, Dad was sitting awake in bed, grieved about my running off and wondering why. He woke her up and demanded to know if she had consciously said something. He told her that she had turned over in her sleep and said loud and clear, not mumbling, "It was God's will!" She had no memory of doing it. She was in a dead sleep. Afterwards, he would not talk about it with her or anyone so far as I know. I am sure that he was still upset, but I hope that this brought him some comfort.

I only spent three and a half years at Elkins High School, but they were formative ones for me. Unlike the huge industrial style setting of the massive Junior High School I attended in Houston, Elkins was a true community school. Everybody knew everybody else. Instead of being shuffled to one room full of virtual strangers to another like it, the same faces showed up again and again. It was not "ethnically and culturally diverse". Just the opposite. There was no racial tension at all because there were no other races. I don't think there was a single African American in the entire school district.

There was one guy from South America who had a Spanish accent. It was eloquent Castilian Spanish and he had a very English first and last name. He barely had an olive cast to his skin. I am pretty sure his family were professional people, not common laborers. I think he's a millionaire now. In our ignorance, but not malice, we called him "Taco". Even if I didn't feel any racial or cultural tension myself, if I was in this large group where plenty of others did then it affected me too. There was none of that for me there.

I found I was much more comfortable in a more intimate setting like that. Large crowds full of strangers and noises put me ill at ease. This was a more relaxed environment which supported the changes which were going on in my sociability. My sister, and stepbrother and stepsister were there before me and had integrated into the school. He was one grade ahead of me and my sister and stepsister were one grade behind. There were also two sisters that I knew from Houston, we had grown up as friends from the crib. Their mother was a friend of my mother and she had also married a man from Northwest Arkansas. They wound up getting a farm that adjoined ours on the back side. So, I already had "connections". I was welcomed by almost everyone from the start.

The one area where I got a less-than-warm reception was from the "Alpha Male" of my class. I will call him "Johnny". He reminded me a bit of Lee. He did not appreciate a potential rival showing up. When he picked on the other kids, I expressed the opinion that it was wrong, challenging his informal "authority". He was plenty willing to fight. Apparently, a few years before there was another kid, since moved off, that was a rival to him. They fought maybe dozens of times, and the other kid usually got the better of him. So, he wasn't afraid of fighting. I thought if it came down to it, I could take him, and of course I wasn't afraid to take a beating either if it went the other way.

He was an amazing fellow really. He had a charismatic personality and was very cunning. He was a "lovable rogue". Maybe I didn't like what he did, but I liked him. To give you an example of how clever and ruthless he was I want to skip ahead in the story. He was elected "Class President" every year from seventh grade to tenth grade. He did this by exploiting the divide between the girls and boys in the class. The girls were drawing attention from older boys and sort of blew off the boys in their own grade and I think this was resented. At any rate, when he gave his speech each year he would openly appeal to the division, saying "we guys need to keep these girls in line" by installing him as President again. The teachers conducting the election were aghast at how openly sexist his pitch was, and the girls in the class were fuming. But they were outnumbered maybe thirty to twenty-five.

His reign ended our Junior year only when through attrition the balance of power shifted, and guys were no longer the majority. It was a tie. The girl running against him pointed out that we had to fund the Jr-Sr. prom and absolutely nothing had been done to prepare for this. She complained that all he did was strut around and act important. After several minutes of going over the record, every word she said true, it was Johnny's turn to speak. He strode to the front of the room with a somber expression and looked at us directly. He said, "If elected, I promise......" and he ended the sentence with a completely irrelevant line from a skit in the previous weekend's "Saturday Night Live" show. Then he sat down to uproarious applause from the guys. It was brilliant.

After several tie votes, one guy decided to break the tie and vote for the responsible choice- the girl. It wasn't me. When the candidates re-entered the room and Johnny saw he had been defeated, he immediately began nominating girls from the "outgroup" for all the other offices. Even though the divisions were not as stark as some places, there was still a larger "in-group" of girls and a somewhat smaller "out-group". Johnny was giving us another lesson in exploiting divisions for political purposes. His revenge was to saddle the girl who beat him with a "cabinet" of girls that she didn't normally socialize with and who may have had a bit of animus against her clique. He split the girl vote and the guys mostly stuck with his nominations (I voted 'split ticket'). In spite of this sabotage, they worked together and did what needed to be done to host a Jr-Sr. prom.

Our senior year, I was the guy nominated for President. The majority girls were not willing to trust any guy, even a Dudley Do-right like me, with the "Big Chair" again. Still, after I lost that election, they immediately nominated me for Vice-President and both sides voted me in. As is usual for that age, the girls showed more maturity than the guys.

Let me now back-track to when I first arrived, and Johnny viewed me as a rival. He turned his wit, and venom, on me. His put-downs were always a lot funnier when directed at someone else! But this time I handled it completely differently than I did with Lee. I had been reading the Bible, and that included Christ's admonition in the Sermon on the Mount to "love your enemies" and "turn the other cheek." I remember specifically when Brandt told me some outrageous thing Johnny said about me that I just answered, "I am sorry to hear he feels that way. I kind of like him and hope we can be friends someday." And I meant it.

Brandt later told me that he repeated my words back to Johnny and that Johnny got embarrassed or maybe even ashamed when he heard them. That didn't happen often with him. It was a lesson in the power of Christ's teachings, when properly applied. Soon after we did become friends, and I guess we still are on some level, though I rarely see anyone I went to high school with now besides my own family.

None of that applied on the football field though. When I showed up as a 177-pound sophomore for two-a-days, a 230-pound senior All-Star nose tackle, who also happened to be the coach's little brother, told me in the locker room, "I can't wait to get you in pads, Moore." I remembered, and a week later when we got pads and had hitting drills I went to the opposite line. I switched places with someone so that I would go against him every time. Each time I hurled myself into him with all of my might. Eventually his brother, the coach, noticed that I was going against him every time and pulled me aside and asked if there was something going on between us. I told him that he had said that he could not wait to get me in pads and I just wanted to make sure that he got enough of it. That's how cocky I was.

It was a different day back then. I know that football is still rough and the athletes are much bigger and stronger now, but we were tough. One year we had two-a-days on a freshly cut hay field. It left thousands of tiny cuts on us. In those days, our "concussion protocol" was to have an assistant coach holler "shake it off" at us. If they were in a good mood, they might respond to an injury by offering the prognosis "It will feel better when it quits hurting." If it was game time, we needed "to learn to tell the difference between pain and injury." Am I exaggerating for effect? Well, maybe. On some of it.

Around that time, I became a pacifist, at least off the football field. That's how seriously I took my new life. And there were several times where I did literally have to "turn the other cheek". Fortunately, no one who hit me took up the offer to land another blow. I continued this to the early part of my college days. In fact, I had signed up for a "War Games" class with the ROTC and at some point, I had to drop the class because pacifists were not allowed to take it. I chose to drop the class rather than renounce pacifism, but not before we had our first war game and our "Confederates", led by me and my buddy Dunn, crushed the Union forces in a tabletop recreation of the Battle of Pea Ridge. In real life the Union had crushed the Confederates.

Communication with my father was restored somewhere near the end of high school. It was he who convinced me to drop pacifism, pointing out that in Revelation, when Christ returns "the blood will be up to the horse's bridle." And my pastor at that time, John Barry Baker, gave a scenario where I come upon a drunk man beating a five-year-old girl. I ask him to stop but he persists. What does the law of love suggest that one do? So sometime in college I realized that turning the other cheek was meant to be a practice, but not an absolute. I renounced pacifism as a philosophy.

I should also add that my senior year of High School I was voted "Friendliest" guy by the other students in the school. My sister Jill was voted "Friendliest" girl and we had our picture taken in the yearbook together. I had changed, or perhaps "been changed" is a more precise way to put it, an immense amount in those three and a half years. I came to Elkins public schools as an anti-social kid with a minor history of violence. I left a pacifist who was voted "Friendliest". Getting to be that person was not an easy process for me.

I was used to having a room, indeed a house, to myself most of the time. We had a large house even for six people, and that didn't bother me. But then my folks started inviting other people who were having some trouble to come live with us. It started with a young man in church whose family wanted him to have a better environment than they could provide. Then another troubled youth. Then some folks we knew in Texas also decided to move to Arkansas, and the four of them moved in with us while their house was being built. Then another couple that was having financial troubles came. At one point, I think twenty-two people were living under our roof.

It was driving me crazy. Some of those people were "hard to love." Mom pointed out to me that anybody can love the loveable. Only those with a heart like God's can love people who are unlovable. She seemed to forget that a year before I didn't even want to have lovable people bothering me except in small doses! I went through a crash-course in how to share, love, and get along with people, even annoying ones. I didn't make straight "A's", that's for sure, but I think I learned something.

Another lesson she taught me was related to the holiness aspect of our theology. Basically, we are born with a sin nature and we agree it needs to be put to death and instead live the new life we have in Christ with a renewed mind. But we can't do this in our own strength. The Holy Spirit has to do it in us. Therefore, these things that vex and annoy us, the trials we all go through, have lessons in them. God wants us to learn something or change something about ourselves in order to "walk in the Spirit". The quicker we repent and give up whatever bad attitude or practice that we have, the more quickly we can learn the lesson. If we don't, we will have to "repeat the lesson" and suffer more. This was actually a powerful method of improvement and coping.

This helped me try to find the lesson in all experiences and just see them all as tests. That set me on a constant path of improvement, even though at the time I still didn't get how much I needed improving! If you learn quickly to quit fighting what life, and the Holy Spirit if you are a believer, wants to teach you, then you can quickly admit when you are in error. You can change course before the consequences get too great. Keep doing that for thirty years, and you will find that you won't be in error nearly as much.

Eventually, things thinned back out in the house and it was just the six of us again. Even still, my mother would cook a huge Sunday feast for everyone who wanted to come to our house after services at the small church we attended. She was cooking for twenty-something people every Sunday. There were that many people there every Sunday. Heck, one young man liked her spaghetti the best, so no matter what else she made on Sunday, she always also made spaghetti for his sake. That's just how hard she tried to be accommodating. Obviously, she modeled a lot of good behavior for me in the "how to not be a selfish jackass" department.

I had a lot more to learn than just that. For a while I was popular with girls. But even that faded as I went through the limited supply and one or the other of us figured out that we were not right for each other pretty quickly. The truth was that I was a straight-laced nerd trapped in (at that time) a jock's body. Just like the actor who played "The Fonz" was nothing like the Fonz, my core was very different from my superficial personality.

While I was a Christian, I was clueless on how to treat girls and listen to them. I mostly didn't mind losing them, but at the end of the road I did lose one I really wanted. I think she wisely realized we were heading two different directions and chose a suitor who was pursuing her harder. I was at an extreme competitive disadvantage because I had no feel for mind-games or subtle signals. I had to develop all that from scratch. Also, I would not lie, or even exaggerate, whereas a lot of guys would tell a girl anything and convince themselves they meant it at the time. I was always aware of future consequences.

In addition to those travails, the little independent church we were trying to build started to lose its luster for me. Eventually I saw the pastor, the man who baptized me in the river, as a control-freak who was in it for himself and didn't really know much about God. I told him when I graduated school that I was going to attend elsewhere. He didn't mind. He knew I was onto him, and five years later the rest of the family would be too. I went to a bigger church in Fayetteville and found a guy named John Barry Baker to be my pastor, but that's another chapter. The main point is that I learned early that church authority figures weren't necessarily legitimate. My attempt to find a human authority to trust was once again frustrated. God was good. The folks that come in His name? You better watch them.

Since I turned eighteen before the election, as a senior in high school I voted for the first time in the election of 1980. My polling place was Sulphur City Baptist Church. There really was no "City" there. Just that church and the abandoned ruins of an old one-room schoolhouse. Most of "my people " were drawn to Ronald Reagan, and so was I. I voted for a guy named Frank White for Governor, who shocked the political world, including himself I think, by upsetting a young hotshot Governor named Bill Clinton.

Two years later, when Bill Clinton earned the name "Comeback Kid" by promising everyone he would be good if we just gave him another chance, I voted for him for the only time in my life. I bought his argument that White wasn't being kind enough to the Cuban Refugees, which was kind of the "tiebreaker" for my vote.

I remember telling my dad in Texas how I thought Reagan was going to win Arkansas. He laughed. He was shocked when I turned out to be right. At that time Arkansas was a thoroughly Democrat state except for the Northwest Corner where I lived. The divide went all the way back to the Civil War. The rugged hills of the Ozarks weren't much for growing cotton, or much else. There were very few slaves. The rest of the state had a lot of farming and saw things differently.

When Arkansas voted to secede from the Union, the Northwest Delegation voted against it. The power brokers asked for one more vote so that it would be unanimous, and the state could present a united front going to war. One delegate, the one from these parts, would not change his vote. His name was Isaac Murphy. He must have been very unpopular in that room. I am sure he was told that any political ambitions he might have were over. He stuck to what he thought was right anyway.

After the North won the war, they imposed Reconstruction Governments on the South, headed by out-of-state guys. Only Arkansas got a native Governor, because they trusted Isaac Murphy. Like a lot of southerners, I have mixed feelings about the Civil War. The slavery was abhorrent and should have been abolished, but generally I don't think the issue of whether a state has the right to secede from a political union should be resolved by violence. But I don't have mixed feelings about Isaac Murphy. I admire and relate to Murphy. He tried to heal the wounds during his time in office, but it was beyond him.

At any rate, the general feeling around Northwest Arkansas was that we were politically isolated from the rest of the state. When I was in High School, besides the University the place was mostly poor hill people. Wal-Mart and Tysons et al were just starting to take off. The rest of the state may have cut our region out of the political spoils, but back then we were too poor to have much to loot.

As we got more prosperous than the rest of the state, there was a period where I felt like the Democrats who ran things were using the Republican Northwest like an ATM machine. Due to the magnetic personality of Bill Clinton, and the fierce loyalty, to a fault really, that Arkansans had for their political tribe, Arkansas was the last southern state to flip to the Republicans. But I get ahead of myself in this story, let me return to those years that shaped me.

My shaping and conditioning had one other major component. Except for a brief period when my father was down after the divorce, I had never really known want. It was the same when I went to Arkansas. During high school we were one of the better-off families around. My stepfather was a contractor, building houses in Northwest Arkansas. He was prosperous, but he was worried about interest rates. They were rising, and it was getting harder for people to afford homes. He struggled with whether he should continue to build "spec houses". That is, houses for which a buyer had not been found, but which he speculated could easily be sold. Encouraged by the "pastor" we had at the time, he rolled the dice and built them.

It was a disastrous move. Almost no one could afford houses with interest rates so high. To make it much worse in Arkansas, there was a "Usury" law which limited interest rates to 10%. Well, once rates went higher than that, mortgage money disappeared from the state almost overnight. Why loan it out in Arkansas for 10% interest when a bank could send the money somewhere else where it could get twelve or fifteen percent? My stepfather got stuck with six spec houses he couldn't sell, and he had borrowed to build them. The law had been a populist one designed to help people. But it ignored economic reality, which is above human legislation. It was my first real lesson in the unintended consequences of laws, and it was a very painful one.

By the end of high school, the family finances were starting to crack. They were slow to reduce spending in response to the income decreasing. Between my junior year of high school and my sophomore year of college we went from being well off to wondering every week if we could pay for groceries. We knew we couldn't pay the loans. I remember one time a sheriff's deputy came by looking for something we owned to take against the liens on our property. I was the only one home and I gave him a Limited-Edition Winchester 30-30 rifle that my grandfather had left me. My stepfather felt terrible about it and went to the sheriff's office and got the rifle back in exchange for some of our furniture.

I would say it took twenty years of hard work to recover, but the truth is we never recovered. Even after the bankruptcy wiped out the debt but not the shame. It was a hard lesson I learned about living within one's means and avoiding excessive speculation, debt, and leverage- as well as the unintended consequences of legislation.

Fact is, interest rates came down once inflation was reduced. The stupid usury law was repealed. By then it was too late for my stepfather. If he had found a way to hang on, he would have been an established contractor in an area of the country that was going to have almost explosive growth for the next two or three decades. For the next twenty-five years in northwest Arkansas, any decent housing contractor could make a pile of money. We would have been very wealthy. And I would have been set up in a profitable business, never having known what it was like to be poor. I would have "been born on third and thought I hit a triple" as someone said of George W. Bush.

I could have been an arrogant jerk without much empathy for the less fortunate. Maybe some cunning gal would have finagled me into marriage for the wrong reasons, with disregard for the fact that I was a little different and I needed a partner who was a little different. Instead, I would walk another path. A harder one, but one more suitable for me. Missing out on all that seemed like misfortune at the time. The pain was very real, but looking back, many of God's blessings come in disguise.

Chapter Three

The Man from Thunder Mountain

I was the first generation of my family to complete college. I attended the University of Arkansas in Fayetteville. It was the state's flagship university. It wasn't fun. I didn't really make any lifelong connections. I barely dated, much less found my soulmate. It was a much prettier setting, but the ant-hill type congestion and constantly shifting faces reminded me more of my junior high years. My world got bigger, and it took me a while to get bigger. I liked people now, but I was still an introvert who just happened to have a big personality. Crowds still drained me.

My family was going through the bankruptcy, and I probably didn't have any business going to college anywhere. But my testing and grades were good enough to basically pay for tuition and books, and with my family's suddenly low income, grant money was available so that I could eat if I watched my pennies. Partying and eating out was not in the budget. For a place to stay, I took a job as the resident custodian of the Presbyterian and Disciples of Christ campus center on Maple Street, right on the campus. They had a one-room apartment in the back.

My father in Texas took care of my transportation. He bought me a new, loaded Pontiac Grand Prix as a high school graduation gift. He also let me set up an account at a local gas station owned by some folks back in Elkins. I commuted from Elkins that first year and stayed in the Center for basically all the rest of it. That meant my junior year the right thing to do was to use the income of my father in Texas to determine my eligibility for grants. That wasn't the best news he ever got, but he never suggested that I keep using my mother and stepfather's income to claim financial aid. He paid the balance of what I lost in grant money that junior year.

He also paid my legal fees. I found out that I could feel fear and sickness. My freshman year of college as I was commuting in from Elkins, I hit a little girl getting off a school bus. I can still see her bouncing along the road as I felt absolutely helpless. I thought I might have killed her. By the grace of God, I didn't. I did break her leg though and it was an emotionally trying time, both the guilt of what I had done and the lengthy trial process.

I was eventually found not guilty. The bus had died in the road at that spot and there was some question as to whether the flashing stop lights were working. To this day, I am not sure. Our insurance company settled with the girl's mother. She told me "I tried to hate you, but everyone I talked to said you were a good young man." I hope that child grew up to have a happy life, with no ill effects. All of that was going on my first two years of college.

Football was no longer a release for me. I had tried to walk-on for the Razorbacks, but they didn't even want me as a walk-on. It was the right call. Honestly, I might have been quality depth at the Division II level. I had no business being out there with either my football prowess or the overall situation. I was in survival mode. I had walked on at two hundred and four muscular pounds. Most kids gain weight when they go to college between beer and no PE, but away from my mom's amazing cooking for the first time, and on my scant budget and with everything we were going through, I lost twenty-two pounds my first year away from home. That was without even trying. At the end of my sophomore year of college I weighed less than I did at the start of my senior year of high school. I don't know that I had more than two beers the whole time I was in college.

The resident custodian job at the Campus Presbyterian and Christian center gave me my first exposure to left-wing Christianity. I remember not being impressed. It would take a long time before I became unimpressed with attempts from the right to harness the church for political action, but it was a start. I would not say that I was a great custodian, but I did help the Director bring that center back to life.

When I first took the job, basically no students hung out there. It was like a tomb. There was this one guy I will call "Michael" who lurked there by himself. He wasn't a student. He was drugged out of his mind and may have been homeless. He couldn't put three sentences together that made any sense. The rumor around town was that he burned down another church. A policeman once told me that he was the #1 suspect in an incident where someone broke into a church, defecated in the large ceremonial bible in front of the pulpit, and wiped himself with the flags on either side of the stage. I guess I don't have to tell you he was crazy.

At first, when no one else used the center, the Director tolerated his presence during the day. When it was time to lock up, it was my job to search the center thoroughly to make sure Michael wasn't hiding anywhere so that he would get locked in overnight. For example, I would turn on the light switch in one of the obscure rooms in the basement, and there he would be, sitting in the corner of a completely dark room. Sometimes he didn't want to leave either. I remember throwing a chair across the room to emphasize to him that it was time to go.

He may have been crazy, but he was not stupid. One night he left the bathroom window unlocked. When I threw him out, he simply waited for me to go to bed, then snuck back in. He then broke into the kitchen downstairs and ate all the church's lunch meat and drank all the communion wine. The Director wasn't too happy when he opened the fridge the next day for the service and it was all gone.

After that I knew to check the locks on the windows. Once I noticed it was unlocked and I left it that way, but waited. I walked in and found him with one leg sticking inside the window trying to get in. I stopped him, but even during regular hours he was a nuisance. Naturally, he regularly left a mess.

The Director finally got tired of showing misplaced charity and instructed me to tell Michael that he could not come back. We were starting to collect some students who were participating. I participated too and became friends with some of them. The place was getting some life to it, and Michael was more a creature of the darkness. He made the students uneasy and they made him uneasy.

I was mowing the lawn when he walked up, wearing a dress and make-up. I told him what the Director said. "But I am a goddess. I create things" he protested. "I made these flowers" he added, indicating the dandelions that I was about to mow down. "That doesn't matter," I retorted, "You don't clean up after yourself." He shot back, "I'll be cleaning up after you for a million-billion years!" Then he stormed off.

He disappeared. After college I heard from a guy in law enforcement that some police who were tired of dealing with him bought a one-way bus ticket to Georgia and told him he was getting on the bus. Supposedly, for extra persuasion they put a gun in his mouth. The guy said that later the Atlanta police kept calling the Fayetteville Police Department saying that they had this crazy guy here who keeps talking about Fayetteville, Arkansas. This fellow told me they denied ever hearing of him. But even after that I heard his name on the radio. It seems he had found his way back to Fayetteville and stabbed some poor old woman to death.

I did date some in my college years, but I felt like something was missing and no romantic relationship lasted more than six months. All kinds of ideas were coming into my head. I was getting a "life of the mind" that I was not born into and it was changing me. I was becoming what I am now, "a nerd trapped in what used to be a jock's body".

As someone, especially a now poor someone, who preferred smaller, more intimate gatherings talking about deep subjects, I didn't fit in with the party scene. I felt like I had little social access to many of the girls on campus. This was so even while there was a huge sorority house right across the narrow alley/sidewalk of the Campus Presbyterian Center where I lived and worked. I lived next door, but they didn't even know who I was.

This was brought out very clearly one evening when I was trying to shut the place down. A rock I had used to prop the doors open became stuck under one of the doors. I went downstairs and got an axe from our storage locker and started using the flat end to break up the rock so I could close the place. The girls next door called the cops and said, "Someone is trying to break into the church next door with an ax." They had no idea who I was, even though I was their neighbor.

Soon a face peered around the corner at one end of the alley. I would soon learn the first face belonged to a police detective. Then uniformed policemen, complete with a dog, showed up on the other end. Then they ordered me down and moved in. I complied. They cuffed me and grilled me for quite a while, I presume while half the sorority was looking at the scene out of their windows. Finally, they let me go when they realized that I worked there and had been living there for over a year. No one from there apologized, probably because I knew none of them and none of them knew me. That's just how invisible I was on that campus.

I did organize a couple of flag football teams during my time there, but flag football just wasn't the same sport for a guy who thirsted for contact due to more testosterone than good sense. The closest I came to political involvement was really just a scheme to get a better flag football team. The intramural handbook said that the members of a team had to have some organizational connection, such as being in the same fraternity, dorm, or student organization.

Well, once I saw how easy it was to start a "student organization" I floated the idea of starting one. Since some of the guys were white boys from my hometown and the others were some black guys from south Arkansas that we met on campus, I figured I could start a club to support "racial harmony." But of course, I didn't care anything about promoting racial harmony, I was just a nineteen or twenty-year-old kid who wanted to win flag football games.

Anyway, the one sticking point was finding a faculty sponsor. I scheduled a meeting with the professor who ran the Black Studies department, Dr. Williams. Before the meeting I realized that he was going to ask me why I wanted to start the club. Rather than cancel the meeting at the last minute I just decided to go in and confess. I admitted to him that I wasn't really an agitator for racial harmony, we had just met some guys that were another color and needed to start an organization to have our own flag football team.

To my shock, he let out an audible sigh of relief. He said forming a club to change a world that didn't want to change wouldn't do any good, but he approved of what I was doing. If that was what it was about, then he wanted to sponsor the organization! The whole thing fell apart anyway when I had a temporary spat with one of the guys. I can't even remember what it was about. But on paper, I ran this "Student Organization" for a year or two.

It was about this time that I had my first real lesson in the power of the media to shape perceptions. A large waste management company was planning a waste dump in the hills south of Elkins where I grew up. I studied the issue with greater interest than I studied my business classes and determined that the geology there was very unfavorable for a waste dump. It was largely fractured and porous limestone, with lots of natural springs and a high water table. I was convinced that sooner or later the clay containment they were touting would fail and the garbage would contaminate the local water table. Most residents of the area, including us until recently, relied on individual wells for our household water.

I was hardly an environmentalist, but I thought this was absurd. I decided to attend the quorum court meeting where the issue was to be discussed. When I arrived, I saw protestors out front with signs, about ten of them. I walked in the doors and found that the building was so packed with people that one could not even enter the room where the meeting was being held. Even the lobby was so full of people that I felt claustrophobic. They were listening to the proceedings over a speaker. They could not see them. It was a massive turnout of citizens who were also opposed to the waste dump.

I decided to go outside and hold a protest sign instead of trading elbows with the thick crowd. Soon a media van pulled up and a reporter from the television station came by and interviewed a couple of us. As I mentioned, I had done my homework and was able to give articulate and reasoned answers as to why the area selected was a poor choice for a large waste dump.

That evening someone called me and told me that I was on the six o'clock news on a certain station. They raved about how well I presented. I had missed it, but I figured they would run the same story at ten o'clock and I would catch it on that same station then.

Ten o'clock came and I watched the news. They had the story of the protest, but by then I wasn't in it. Between six and ten o'clock the story changed. I wasn't on the ten o'clock version. Instead, the announcer showed the handful of people outside the building and said, "About a dozen people showed up to protest the proposed waste management facility". They did not mention that the entire hearing room and lobby was also packed with people who were against it! And instead of me giving articulate, well-reasoned answers, they showed some poor fellow from the back woods. They asked him, "Have you ever been to a protest before?" He said, "Nope." They asked, "Why are you here now?" He answered, "Don't want the dump." I was floored at how completely they could change the narrative in just four hours.

It was also during that time that there was a lot of news coverage about events in El Salvador. They were having their first semi-free and fair election. There were many parties running. One of them was "ARENA", headed up by a former Army Major named Roberto D'Aubuisson. It was widely believed that D'Aubuisson was behind what the media called "right-wing death squads" in El Salvador. Even Archbishop Oscar Romero was said to be among his many victims. The way the media painted him, it seemed absurd to believe that anyone except a few of the richest landowners who fanatically hated communism would support him. It was said he used blowtorches to interrogate people. He seems to have been a psychotic murderer. That is certainly how he was portrayed, though he always denied the chargers, and so far as I know none of them were ever proven in a court of law.

What was never explained in the U.S. media coverage was why any significant slice of the electorate might want to vote for him. Thus, I assumed that his formation of a political party was a part of his general madness. Certainly, that was the impression of his chances that one would have gotten from watching media coverage of his campaign from the big networks in the United States.

It was then that a funny thing happened. They had the actual election, and ARENA finished with more votes than any other party. ARENA was not isolated from all the other parties either. It wasn't the case that ARENA only got the most votes because those against ARENA split the vote. Instead, ARENA and the parties allied with ARENA won a majority of seats in the Constituent Assembly, their version of Congress. D'Abussion became the President of the Assembly. I could only conclude that most El Salvadorans preferred "Right-Wing" death squads to Communist Death Squads, even if the Yankee media never did any reporting on the latter.

Between that and the Waste Dump experience, I quit believing the story I was told by the media, local or global. It was a decision which has been confirmed and re-confirmed as the wise choice many, many times since. Eventually I developed "Moore's Media Maxim": *The establishment media does not exist to inform the public. The establishment media exists to protect the establishment.* Later, after the bail-outs, I would also have a second media maxim: *Any nation with corporations too big to fail is going to have an establishment media that is too connected to the system to Tell You the Truth.*

Some readers may consider my judgement to have been too rash. Unfortunately, events proved that my skepticism about the system and its narratives still wasn't deep enough. For example, D'Aubuisson was narrowly defeated in the next election for President of the Republic of El Salvador by a man named Duarte. D'Aubuisson accused him of being a tool of the American CIA. It was easy to dismiss as sour grapes from a crazy guy, but later it turned out that Duarte was indeed a CIA asset.

But it got worse. The "Reverend" Louis Farrakhan, leader of the cultic "Nation of Islam" was, during the same period, accusing the CIA of bringing drugs into the United States and poisoning poor black neighborhoods. I thought he was a nut job. The charge was laughable. Well, he may be a nut job, but years later we found out about Barry Seal and the Mena Arkansas airport. This wasn't the CIA directly, but their agents were in fact bringing massive amounts of narcotics into the country with their help. It turned out that just being outside of my mental category of "people in groups I like" wasn't enough to dismiss someone as wrong. I needed to listen more, as most of us do.

Unfortunately, back on the college front I was on average a "B" student. In high school I didn't have to work for it...except for algebra which I never got in high school. I didn't really get it in college either, but I had a knack for statistics and economic math. At any rate, I was not as driven as some of my peers, nor did I have the good work habits that some of my peers had. It got better as I went and by the end of it, I was pulling "all-nighters" too, but it took a while for me to adjust. This did not apply to things I was interested in, which I threw myself into with abandon.

When my grades (and interest) in science classes were higher than my grades in most of my business classes it should have been a clue for me that I was cut out for something other than business. My family was in business, so I went into business. But then the coding classes came along. My actual major was in "Data Processing and Quantitative Analysis". I was naturally gifted at writing computer programs and understanding how systems fit together. Doing it only further sharpened my mind and logic skills. I was better than average, but I wasn't a whiz. And while I didn't like crowds, I found out that I liked people. Being locked in a room all day to code only appealed to me on some days.

Our equipment was so antiquated that one of our courses even used cardboard punch cards to feed the program code into the computer. Personal computers were almost unknown, but I had a Commodore VIC Twenty. It was an eight-bit computer with no hard drive, and of course no internet, which hooked up to a TV screen. It was hard for universities to keep up with the changes going on in the field.

I started going to church in town, but as was typical for me I didn't go where the other college kids hung out. I went to a big independent church that very few students went to. I spent a lot of time in the office of the Associate Pastor, John Barry Baker. He had some of that "life of the mind" that I was thirsty to experience. He was an attorney who quit the practice of law and became a minister.

As a young man, he professed atheism, and was converted after he was convinced that God moved in his life in a real way. He was the youngest Prosecutor in the state of Arkansas at one time. Years later he told me that almost by accident he had found himself an "insider". He gave me a definition of "insider" that stuck with me. He said, "To be an insider, when the chips are down you have to be willing to do the wrong thing for the right people." He got off that fast track. The Bakers had six kids and they were the first people I ever met who homeschooled, at least for their younger children. He will come back into the story later.

The summer after my junior year of college, I went to Houston to spend time with my dad. He was prospering in the real estate business with his own "Century 21" franchise. I watched him operate after my sophomore year of college, when I had also visited him. He made a lot of money and he made it look effortless. His touch was so light it might not be apparent to people that he was managing them. He'd just have friendly visits with people and have a talk. At the end of the talk, they'd decide to do something differently without ever being given a directive. He "worked" maybe three hours a day most days. When I pointed this lax schedule out to him, he told me "Son, I did my hard work getting this job."

It taught me the value of working smarter rather than harder. The truth is, I've worked a lot harder on some of my lower paying jobs than I have on my higher paying ones. There is a lot to finding out who you really are and doing that, finding that natural fit. Part of working smarter was not giving up on people. He had this agent who made crude comments to the female employees. Today it would be considered sexual harassment, but back then it was just being a jerk. When I suggested in private that he fire the guy he told me, "Anyone can fire someone. It takes no leadership or management skills at all." He was going to handle it his own way. I left for the year soon after that, but I figure the guy shaped up after a visit where he thought it was his own idea to change his behavior.

Not a Good Summer

At any rate, I was looking forward to a great Summer getting to know my father better as an adult. I had left when I was fourteen and he didn't see me again until I was eighteen, and then just for a couple of months in the Summer. I was becoming his friend and not just his son.

I think I mentioned that my dad had type one diabetes. He wasn't supposed to have lived past forty. He did, he was fifty-four when he died, but his body was betraying his spirit. He had a club foot and walked with a cane, but still had "presence." He knew his days were numbered and had made his peace.

He had a little incident almost as soon as I got there. Afterwards he was resting in bed. He called me to his bedside and said that he might not live too much longer. He said that Essie was a young mother and needed the help, and he could only leave my sister Jill and me $5,000 each. I told him that was enough. But I also protested that I wanted him to see me as a man. I wanted him to see me do great things. He said that he would be watching from heaven. I objected that then I was afraid that he would see too much. That is when he told me, "I will turn my head the other way son, I promise." I like to think that this is a shadow of what our heavenly Father does for those who trust Him.

The next day he was up and around, and I was optimistic that he was recovering. Unfortunately, the fourth day I was there, he collapsed on his bedroom floor due to heart failure. My stepmother Essie, who was trained as a nurse, immediately began CPR. She brought him back but in the middle of it she jumped up and said, "he bit my tongue!". They got him to the hospital and put him on life support. She later amplified to me that it seemed like he was resisting, like he didn't want to be brought back.

Essie and I went to his bedside in intensive care. He could not speak. He was fading fast. She questioned him about biting her tongue, as if he did not want to come back. She held his hand and said, "Did you see Jesus? Squeeze my hand if you saw Jesus." He squeezed her hand. He motioned for a pen and paper. She got one but put it in his left hand. He tried to write something out anyway. He was very determined, but he could not write legibly. We never knew what he wanted to say about his experience, but we knew he was ready to go. The order was given, and the machine was turned off. He moved to the next life.

He may have been ready to go, but I was not ready for him to go. People express grief differently, and with me it was with anger. I flew into a violent rage, pounding on walls and doors and anything in sight. Finally, I collapsed in the corner. After that, a security guard walked in. He could see how I was grieving, and I guess he didn't want to make an issue of my behavior since I seemed to be done. I am glad he did not walk in a few minutes earlier with some kind of attitude. That wouldn't have turned out well for anybody. Just one of the many lucky breaks I realize I got along the way.

I stayed for the funeral, and then I went back to Arkansas. As Essie said when she looked in the coffin and saw his body, "that's just the cocoon. The butterfly has flown." I was twenty.

I had one year of college left to go. I had the $5,000 he had left me, my job at the center to put a roof over my head, a $500 student loan, and some work-study money from shelving books in the library. I had to watch my pennies closely, but by the end of that Summer, I had a bachelor's degree in Business Administration. I was flat broke. Thus, began my real adulthood.

Chapter Four

An Officer and a Gentleman

Our professors had assured us that though Data Processing and Quantitative Analysis was a tough degree, if we got it then we could "write our own ticket" or words to that effect. Fact is, I went through interviews, but never got an offer from private business. There was a dip in demand for programmers around the time I graduated. Demand would return a year or two later when it was too late to help me. My family had zero connections. They were still barely hanging on.

While I was waiting for my luck to change, I had to get a job delivering pizza. My life after graduation was quite a let-down. This was pretty humiliating for a guy who thought he was going to be a big-time computer programmer making lots of money just before that. Hey, I was probably too cocky and needed some humbling, but it still hurt.

One place that was hiring was the U.S. Military. Once I rejected pacifism, I had always thought that the military would be a good experience to help a lot of people grow up- I just didn't think I'd be one of them. But it turned out I needed a grown-up job, so I went into the recruiting offices and started making inquiries. Ronald

Reagan had made being in the military "cool" again, after a tough dip in public perception following the Vietnam War.

My first choice was the Navy, which was trying to expand to six hundred ships. I wasn't a sissy obviously, but I wasn't one of those guys who thought crawling through the mud with a knife in my teeth looking for someone to kill was my cup of tea. The idea of seeing more of the world appealed to me, as well as the fact that the ships were a massive integrated capital investment. I had no idea what I was getting into, but they sold me on applying for "Supply Officer" aboard a ship, which is kind of like running a business.

As the process went on, they called me to Little Rock and said there were no openings for Supply Officers. I asked why they had asked me there if there were no such openings, and what my options were. They offered me a chance at a commission to be a Surface Warfare Officer. A "ship driver", just what you think of when you think of the Navy. I said, "Well, on the plus side, at least I would get to wear the uniform." For once I gave the right answer. It turned out I'd have rather been a Surface Warfare Officer than a Supply Officer anyway. I just didn't know it at the time, because I literally knew nothing about the Navy, or operating a ship. I didn't know what you called the blunt end from the pointy end.

I was ordered to report to Officer Candidate School in Newport, Rhode Island. Meanwhile I delivered Pizzas and brooded. Rhode Island was like another world. I missed everything about home. My habits were far from military. They were looking to weed out any weak links. But the hardest thing about it was the teaching style.

Decades after this an observant friend of mine who had seen me operate up close for a while said, "The hard things are easy for you and the easy things are hard." That was a great way to put it, at least concerning some hard things. Other hard things are also hard for me. But my strength was always analysis and making connections that were not obvious. Call it "analytical creativity." I did best when someone started with the big picture and then explained how all the pieces tied into it. Sometimes this means that it takes me a little longer to get the details than it does other people, but once I get them, look out.

Well, everything in Officer Candidate School in Newport Rhode Island was the opposite of that. It has aptly been described as "drinking from a firehose." It seemed like every other day they would plop another manual on your desk and say, "memorize this." It may have been about some details of boiler operation, or personnel administrative paperwork. No context was given for any of it. It was just the mass-memorization of seemingly unconnected facts. This was the way enlisted personnel became officers, or those who were from Navy families, so the classes were loaded with people who had context for all of this. I just wasn't one of them. In addition, those Yankee germs kicked my tail. I spent a lot of time struggling with minor sicknesses. Physically it wasn't challenging at all. In fact, I often sought extra exercise on my own.

I confess to you that I almost didn't make it out of there with a commission. The officers running the place held an inquiry and grilled me. They decided to hold me back and have me retake the first eight weeks. They did not send me home in failure. There were two things in my favor. My peer-evals were generally favorable and my grades on watch were superior. I could think on my feet a lot better than I could think on my rear end. In particular when the rear-end thinking was laid out in the way in which I was academically weakest. Somehow, I made it out of there with a commission, and was ready to get my first assignment.

In theory, we had some leeway as to our billeting (the job we were assigned). I requested a combatant as my top priority. If I was going to be a "Surface Warfare Officer", I at least wanted to be on a warship and not a tender or supply ship. My next priority was homeport. Basically, I just wanted to get back to the South. On the east coast, which is where our real options were, there were pretty good-sized Naval bases in Mayport Florida and in Charleston,

South Carolina. Then of course there was the huge one in Norfolk Virginia. I put down those three in that order. Newport, Rhode Island, the same place they had Officer Candidate School, also had a tiny Navy Base with maybe four frigates, an obsolete destroyer from the 1950s, and a minesweeper. I didn't put it on my list. Newport was sort of a "glamour" billet for a certain class of traditional Naval person, but I was trying to get out of there!

One by one, each of my classmates got their orders. I was the last one in my class to get them. I wondered what the hold-up was. Those three ports were full of warships. Granted a look at my record so far would indicate that I was one of the dimmer bulbs academically, but I knew that was just an artifact of the way they taught the material combined with my lack of proper background. There were signs that it was starting to "click" for me, and there was little doubt I would be a good shipmate. People even remarked at the time that the delay was very odd.

At last, my orders came through. I was assigned as an Anti-Submarine Warfare (ASW) Officer to the USS Edson, DD-946. That was the obsolete destroyer built in the 1950s that was stationed in Newport, Rhode Island. Somehow, they couldn't find a billet for me on any of those warships in Mayport, Charleston, or Norfolk. I would be assigned to a tour of duty, starting with a billet as ASW Officer on what was known as the Navy's "last all-gun destroyer".

The Edson was built in 1958, before destroyers were typically outfitted with missiles, or for that matter many of the tools necessary to effectively battle submarines of the modern era. I mean, if it is known as the "last all gun destroyer" then the anti-submarine suite was so outdated that it didn't even rate a mention. It would have done well against the Fuhrer's U-boats in 1944, I guess.

Naturally the personnel assigned to my division tended to be those who had not qualified on more modern systems- basically the enlisted version of my academic record at Officer Candidate School. The boilers were a mess and we were the terror of every repair facility on the East Coast. They were all afraid we would steam in and break down, leaving it to them to fix our antiquated boilers and engineering systems for which replacement parts were generally unavailable. Sending us across the Atlantic Ocean on a full deployment with a carrier task force was out of the question. Until we broke down, we would have done well providing shore bombardment for a landing force though. That never happened. Mostly what we did was train reservists from Boston. In fact, the ship was in the yards at Boston when I first got there.

 I don't want to say it was all bad. The lines of the ship were gorgeous. It looked like one of those little British sports cars, not big and boxy like the newer ships. Later in life I took a trip up to Saginaw Michigan where it is in a naval museum and remembered her and those times with affection. And technically, it was the squadron flagship. If someone didn't like to go on long deployments, like say a guy at the end of his career or a Newport homeboy, it was good. Heck on paper it was a toney assignment. It was only when you got a closer look that it became clear that for a young junior officer looking to build his service record, it was a dead end. The Edson was now a career killer that probably should have been decommissioned rather than refurbished one last time.

 Though she served well in Vietnam and was even used in an episode of "The Twilight Zone", by the time I got aboard she was mostly a money pit. Before my tour was up, Washington would realize that too. In the meantime, morale in the enlisted ranks could be summed up by a Petty Officer who looked me in the eye and said, "I took an oath to defend the Constitution from all enemies, foreign and domestic. This ship is a domestic enemy!"

 So, there I was, but I didn't understand how I got here. Once I got settled in and the other junior officers thought I was OK, one of them clued me in on what they thought happened. It turned out that my predecessor, I won't mention his name, was stationed on the ship for maybe six months when suddenly he got re-assigned to a Spruance Class Destroyer, at the time one of our front-line warships, in Norfolk. That basically never happens. Once a Junior officer was assigned to a ship, he served a long tour of duty, two years anyway. His new assignment sounded just like what I had asked for.

It turned out that my predecessor's father was an influential USN Captain stationed in Washington D.C. When I remarked on my situation this fellow officer on my ship revealed all this to me. It was his opinion, and that of some others aboard, that the young man had his father pull some strings once he realized the assignment wasn't the plum that he thought that it was. The billeting officer just had to figure out what loser Ensign would get his orders traded and be stuck there instead. That was me.

We had very cramped and Spartan quarters on the ship, even by shipboard standards. The ship was in the yards in Boston when I first arrived. It took months for it to even get back in the water. We rented housing to live in when not sailing or on Duty Days (about one day out of four when we stayed on the ship 24-hours straight even if it was in port). Officers got the same housing allowance whether they rented a mansion on their own or shared a flop with other officers. I was invited to join in with three other Junior Officers in their rental. A flop with several Junior Officers in it was called a "Snake Pit".

The most senior of the four of us was a tall, friendly Boston area fellow of Scotch-Irish descent I will call "McLarty". I liked him. Another was "Davey", a short, muscular, tightly-wound energetic fellow from Maine I think. The third I will call "Geoff", who was also from the Northeast and had a very awkward and ethnic last name. He was the "Supply Officer" for the ship, so he was the guy doing the job I was originally interested in. He was probably the most obnoxious person I had ever met.

Geoff rarely referred to anyone below him in rank by their proper name. He had nicknames for them all. One of the other Junior Officers told me they once walked in on Geoff while he was going over a list of the crew, trying to come up with demeaning nicknames for all of them. Mine was "Junior". McLarty assured me that it did not fit. My first Thanksgiving up there McLarty and Davey had leave. I was stuck with Geoff and we had to eat out. His behavior was abhorrent. He called the waitress "wench" several times. I was aghast. I doubt that I will ever have a worse Thanksgiving than that one, even if I die on Thanksgiving!

Davey was a bit out there. He brought a motorcycle to the house and showed it to me. Then he asked me if I wanted to ride it. I said "sure". I thought he was going to let me take it for a spin, instead he said, "OK, get on." He wanted me to ride behind him on it. I complied and he took off. On this ride, once in a while he would scream out "Tighter! Hold on tighter!" I figured we were about to hit a bump, so I grabbed him more tightly. I was puzzled that none came. Weird stuff like that.

Later it transpired that Davey was expelled from the Navy due to homosexual activity. The rumor was that he was caught with an enlisted man. I visited him once afterward, but it was awkward.

Eventually the Snake Pit broke up when the ship moved from Boston back to Newport, and I never took more than one roommate at a time after that. Among those room-mates was my good friend John Ahler, an Indiana Catholic boy. Unfortunately for me, he got a better offer for lodging – when he married his fiancé Melissa. He even asked me to come back to Indiana with him to command a "Sword Arch Detail" in his wedding. That was the only leave I didn't use on a visit to Arkansas. When I gave the command to lift swords, I was looking back at the bride's entrance instead of straight ahead, so the point of the sword caught the bill of my cap and sent it flying into the fourth row. I let out a barnyard epithet louder than I meant to. What a dork. They took it well.

I was a bit of a jock and good with people one-on-one, so I was made the Ship's "Welfare and Recreation Officer" as one of my first collateral duties. That meant the guy who hated parties was now a party-planner. We even hosted a British ship. I planned several events at the party, including a Rugby game where they dominated us with their superior skill.

That wasn't all. I decided to have a "Beer Tasting Contest" where five cups of unlabeled beer were on the counter, along with five empty bottles. The idea was to see who could best match them up. Three crew members from each ship were picked to represent their unit. The Americans guzzled their samples and gave haphazard guesses. The Brits never even took a sip. They correctly guessed all five brands simply by comparing colors. I bet they were thinking "How did our ancestors lose two wars to these people?"

Fairly close to the start of my tour, our ship got a new Captain, who was to remain with us throughout. Gideon Wilcox Almy III was the scion of an established Newport family who basically ran off and enlisted in the Navy as a young man. He was rather short and slight of frame, so you might think that he was a bit of a dandy hearing all of this. You would be wrong. He was a tough customer who didn't mind getting his hands dirty. He packed a lot of energy and aggression into that frame of his. He could be rough as a cobb, and he demanded, and got, more than anybody could expect of the crew in that situation.

I served during the Cold War, before a lot of this useless interventionism. We were where we were for a purpose, but there was no shooting going on. Captain Almy would have been great in an actual war. The Navy we had at the time was more of a bureaucracy where mistake-avoidance or deflection was the key to advancement, along with getting the right billets of course. He was willing to take risks, calculated ones anyway.

We never saw combat, but there was a Soviet intelligence gathering ship off the east coast that we gave a very hard time. Once we were steaming with zero visibility due to "pea soup" type fog. We just had our ancient radar to navigate with. He had us make one pass after another toward the blip on the radar that was that ship.

We came so close that any of the passes seemed like they could have resulted in a collision. Someone called us over the ship-to-ship radio and a nervous voice with a Russian accent tried to claim they were a trawler or something. He was practically begging us to break off.

Another time, I think it was the same Soviet ship, not only did we close-pass, but as we broke off, we blew off the soot from our stacks in such a way that the down-wind Soviet vessel was covered in ashes. That one got some attention from the higher-ups I think. One of the other Junior Officers remarked about how the Captain stood out by saying that they should keep him cryogenically frozen with a sign on the case reading, "In case of war, break glass."

Captain Almy didn't let us even see him smile at first. The initial rumor on him was that as someone who worked his way up through the enlisted ranks, he did not like junior officers. A year into it though, he was out drinking with the wardroom and having a good time. He had his "posse". I wasn't one of them. There was a big cultural gap between the older and some of the younger officers on the ship. The Junior Officers signed up after Ronald Reagan made being in the military cool again. The more senior officers on the ship were of that generation which had to hold down the fort during the depressing and wild post-Vietnam era. They thought carousing was the thing to do. I was among the junior officers who went a time or two and then many of us distanced ourselves.

Even though I was not among those officers who went out drinking with the Captain, he still took a liking to me. It was mutual. But then he set me up with his younger daughter. I liked her fine, but I figured out after one date that I did not want to be the guy going out with the Captain's daughter. My history was that pretty quickly one or the other of us would figure out it wasn't the right match. What situation would I be in if that happened after we dated for six months? I was always contemplating future consequences rather than letting my hormones do the thinking. Later he wanted to introduce me to his older daughter who he said was very different from his younger daughter. I was too stupid at the time to realize what an incredible honor it was for him to want to do this. I have a daughter now, and if I try to set her up with some young man, it won't be because I think he is an ignorant hick.

During this time, we were broken down a lot. When we weren't, I'd still be on the ship all week and then we would sail with reservists all weekend. I joined a "Conservative Book Club" and was a voracious reader of books on political theory, history, religion, and science. With no love life and no church life, and no friends outside of work, there was time for it.

We even went to GITMO, the American Base in Cuba, for testing. It was bad enough being on the base as one of the military personnel, I can't imagine how tough it would be to be a prisoner. One time some group brought these models in and set up runways. Hundreds of sailors and Marines were there right up against the runway. I was stuck with Military Police (MP) duty. I had four guys in my detail. Some of those knuckleheads were reaching out and touching the girls, and I was slapping their arms away. But who blames the hungry dogs when people are flashing meat? Those girls were provocative.

When there was a break the event organizer came to me about the touching. I told him that I had four guys to control four hundred and they needed to tone it down. They did and my guys and I moved the sailors and Marines back a couple of steps. It could have ended like that surreal Playboy Bunny scene at the base in the movie "Apocalypse Now". It was a rough place, in fact some of our sailors later got into a brawl with the Marine guards who were stationed there. Marines were coming out the showers wearing a towel and flip flops to get in on it.

Gitmo was an adventure, of sorts. Usually though, our ship was broken down so much that it left me wanting more action. A couple of times I volunteered to sail with other ships who had functioning engineering rooms and modern combat systems. Overall though, I had no chance to excel on the Edson, and I didn't excel. The ship was slated to be decommissioned shortly before my four years of obligated service was over. I had served as ASW Officer, Communications Officer, and Combat Information Center Officer/Assistant Navigator during my time there. I had never planned on making the military a career, and obviously nothing that happened during my time in changed that. I told the detailer that I wanted out. After four years of service home ported in Rhode Island, I was ready to go home.

I gladly said goodbye to Rhode Island and travelled through a blizzard to get to Arkansas as soon as I could. When I got to our old family place on Thunder Road, I saw that my mom had tied 100 yellow ribbons around a tree near the driveway, just like in that old song. I was glad to be back. I still didn't know what I would do. I copyrighted a couple of board games because I was just that much of a nerd by then, but that wasn't my future. The computer world had passed me by in the four years I had spent in the service. I was reduced to menial jobs again while I figured out what I would do.

I soon signed up to actively drill in the Naval Reserve. I had a two-year obligation anyway and there was a tiny reserve base in Fayetteville at the time. I did a lot better as a reservist than I did as active duty. We were assigned to an Aegis cruiser, a front-line ship. And we were the very first reserve unit ever assigned to one. Our readiness level began at literally zero because no one had produced any guidance on what things reservists would have to do on such a vessel to demonstrate their readiness.

Instead of floundering helplessly at this complete lack of guidance, I worked with the enlisted men in my unit to compile some lists and basically write our own readiness requirements. I asked them what specific jobs they would have to do to be ready to maintain the system in their rate. Then I wrote it up into our in-house requirements. It went the other way too. I instructed the guys that when they did their two weeks active duty, they were to ask their chief for something to do related to the work of the division. Any assignment they gave them was added to our in-house list. What they did became what our in-house requirements were. I also emphasized that before they left their two weeks of active duty, our sailors should ask the chiefs on the ship to sign off the tasks they completed from our lists. We did this for each specialty in our unit.

It didn't work perfectly but when the official list came out, we had already done a bunch of the stuff on it. We had made good guesses about what they were going to ask of us, or maybe they took our lists and used them to compile the standards, I am not sure. But by the end of my two years there we were at the second highest readiness level, even though they had just dropped the requirements on us shortly before that. I got a Navy Achievement Medal for that one. I also got a National Defense Service Ribbon in my time in the reserves, though I didn't do anything for it. The first Gulf War happened during this period and the military was very self-congratulatory. I volunteered to go to active duty, but I doubt the request even went up the chain. I didn't have the kind of resume they needed anyway.

I was about to start the next phase of my life, which I will describe in the next chapter, and Bill Clinton was the President-elect. I had to decide if I was going to transfer to another reserve center or resign. I chose to resign my commission. That's how anti-Clinton I had gotten. Now I see that his policies were not so different from those who came before or after him, but at the time I ranted about how I did not want to serve under him. My time as an Officer and a Gentleman had come to an end.

Chapter Five

Educator

When I first got out of the Navy, I was glad to be home, but I had no realistic plans. I got a job at the Sheriff's Office as a Dispatcher. I didn't get along there because I couldn't or wouldn't keep my mouth shut about some of the way they did business.

To give you an example, dispatchers often had to call tow trucks to get a vehicle moved. There was a short list of favored tow-truck operators we were supposed to call. One day this soft-spoken clean-cut guy maybe a little younger than me came into the dispatcher's office. Imagine a wholesome looking and acting version of George Throughgood, the musician who sang "Bad to the Bone."

He had come by in person because he had tried to get his wrecker service into the rotation for county business and never seemed to be included, which any wrecker service without a complaint against it should have been able to do. I added his name to the list and called him the first time there was a need for a tow in his area. That young man was Jim Bob Duggar, many years later of "Nineteen and Counting" fame. He comes back into the story later, but this was the first time I ever met him. I could tell my supervisor didn't like my adding him to the list, they had ones they

Educator

liked getting all the business, but the guy was a taxpayer too and was within his rights.

Honestly, some of them thought I was an FBI agent planted there to spy on them. One of them even asked me point-blank if I was. I just said, "If I deny it you are not going to believe me anyway." As soon as they figured out that I wasn't, they canned me. I was devastated that I couldn't hold onto even a relatively modest job like that. The next election, the voters fired that administration by voting for the outsider candidate, so maybe they should have listened.

I think after that is when I got the job boxing books for minimum wage. This was also about the time of my 10th high school reunion. I was single with no prospects and working a minimum wage job. And my boss at the warehouse had some connection to the school and he was going to be there too. I was dreading it.

It turned out fine, except that we could not persuade Johnny to come. More than one of us asked. He told a couple of us that he would, but didn't show. Nor did he show when we all went to the lake the next day and asked him again. I say "we all" but the truth is that drugs swept through that school my junior and senior year. Half the kids did drugs and the other half did not. Of those who showed up for our tenth reunion, everyone there was from the half that did not do drugs in High School. There is a lesson in there somewhere.

I also dabbled in politics in a serious way for the first time. The church I had gone to before I left for the Navy was in terminal decline. John Barry Baker, the associate pastor who I visited so much before, was the pastor now, but he inherited an impossible situation. A giant facility with a small congregation was not sustainable. It was a lesson in how big facilities, so impressive when things were going well, could be an albatross in tough times. Since they were independent, it wasn't like he could transfer. He tried going back to law. Pretty quickly, he decided to run for Circuit

Judge, which was an elected position in that state. I put up signs, figured who we should mail, and helped get the envelopes stuffed. He wound up narrowly losing, and from there on out stuck to practicing law and preaching on the side at a food kitchen on the wrong side of the tracks- which was sponsored by another large church in the area. I hurt for him. It would not be my last political disappointment.

I tried being a substitute teacher some too. Back then the requirements were pretty lax. I substituted as a Home Economics teacher, as an English teacher. It didn't matter. One day I was a Special Ed teacher. There was a boy in that class named Nathan, and he was in like fifth or sixth grade. He couldn't read a lick. He couldn't read the word "cat". And the only real problem he had that I could see is that he never learned the phonics of the letters. I wound up tutoring him at his home on my own time. That summer, I taught him how to read, and I thought it was one of the best things I ever did.

I wound up getting a job in a resident care facility for troubled youth. They were under lock-down 24-7, unless they had a special pass with escort (guard). The facility included three small classrooms. These kids had been massively screwed over by life at an early age. That's why they were locked up so young.

They would often go wild and we would have to forcibly restrain them and put them in a small padded room for fifteen-minute stretches. We actually had training in how to subdue and transport people without injuring them. And we used that training frequently. Anyway, I wound up gravitating towards the classrooms and after a while spent many days as a teacher's assistant. I also would not hesitate to take them out for a burger or something on my own time as a reward for good behavior, so I quickly became an "inmate favorite".

We admitted one girl in there who some thought we should not have admitted because she had not gotten a clear pregnancy test

Educator

result. A few weeks later, they did test her, and she was pregnant, which meant she would have to leave the facility. She confessed to me why she was leaving and asked, "Mr. Moore what am I going to do?" I told her that it wasn't like she was going to die. People have babies every day. It is just something you go through for nine months, and then you bring a new life into the world. She was visibly relieved. Did I save a life with those few words? To this day I don't know. She transferred out right after that.

By this time, I wanted to teach. I could tell I was good at it and had a passion for it. But my degree was in business administration. My stepbrother was a teacher. My sister was a teacher. I wanted to be a teacher. I had no idea how I would do that. Then one day I went to go see John Hammond, the guy we had ignorantly called "Taco" back in High School. He happened to know about a program for the alternative certification of teachers in Arkansas. You had to take some special training, and maybe a couple of college courses to flesh out your degree, but with a little time and effort someone with a college degree could become a state certified teacher.

I investigated and found out that I was very close to the science hours needed to get a certification for Middle School Science. I took the extra classes, attended the special training, and got a "Provisional" certificate. My siblings did teach but neither was in a position to help me out and so I made a connection-free effort to find a teaching job with only a provisional certificate.

None of the public schools would have me, but there was a tiny Christian school in the nearby city of Rogers that was looking for a science/computer teacher..../chapel coordinator/basketball coach. They offered the princely sum of $16,600 for these services. I had to take it and keep working for a regular certificate. I told them I wasn't a basketball coach, but not only did the principal not seem to mind, but the parent that was in the room during the interview didn't seem to mind either. I will call him "Gary". The principal emphasized to me that the kids were spoiled and pampered. It seemed like he wanted someone who would instill discipline.

There were only seven teachers for grades seven through twelve. There were four basketball teams. I coached the boys junior high and senior high teams. The girls also had teams but thankfully we were able to find a volunteer who would coach them. I was also "Athletic Director" and was over all the teams and scheduling games for them as well. Every boy in grades seven through nine was on the junior high team, although I only had one ninth grader and he had health concerns and was at the end of the bench.

With all I had to do, I barely had a chance to look at the material before classes started. My adrenaline and ability to present and make connections carried me through. I just used the questions that came with the book on my tests, but you would have thought I was killing them the way they carried on about how hard my tests were. I tried to make it as engaging as possible, but I was there to teach and not socialize. Pretty quickly there became two groups. The ones that appreciated what I was trying to do and responded and those who resented it and rebelled. This was reflective of the deeper division in the kind of kids who sought out the school. Some were there because they were super straight-laced and others were there because their parents said "my 16 year-old is broken, here fix him!". It was oil and water.

I also found out why Gary didn't mind me being the basketball coach even though I had no experience and his son was the top player. He wanted to coach the teams, and just have someone around who would do the grunt work. I found him in the gym with the girl's-basketball team after school hours having what was in reality an illegal practice. Our conference rules prohibited after-school practices until the season was close. I told him he shouldn't do that, and it was going to stop- earning an enemy. Meanwhile, the season was drawing closer.

Educator

Fortunately for me my stepbrother was an excellent coach, it didn't matter if the sport was football or basketball. He was teaching junior high in Austin and the team he was coaching lost only one game in two years. He gave me a crash course in coaching a basketball team and it worked. We came out like gangbusters, overwhelming people with a press defense. I found out soon that basketball was taking all my time, because the parents don't all show up to watch you teach science.

My good fortune didn't last though. I had just enough good players to make it work. Then we had a good one who got sick, then another one hurt. The one that got hurt I felt particularly bad about because I had encouraged him to come back for his senior year when he was thinking about leaving the school.

About midway through the season, we started losing and Gary pounced. He convinced someone to donate money to fill the "need" of a new basketball coach and I was relieved of senior high team duties in mid-season for a fellow he knew that did in fact know more basketball than I did. That didn't fix the losses though.

They were 7-5 when I was ousted. I think they won maybe two of the ten or so games left after that. Even when the sick and hurt players came back, they couldn't get it together. It was very difficult for me when they took that senior high team away. In either a startling lack of sensitivity or maybe someone was trying to rub my face in it, after they relieved me, they "suggested" that since I would not have to worry about practice after school anymore that I instead spend the evening going to watch our next opponent play and give them a scouting report. I had to really swallow hard and think about everything Jesus said to do in my spirit, because the rest of me wanted to kick some serious ass.

I went to the game and noticed a few weaknesses in the other team's deployment, and I gave the guy who replaced me my report. To his credit he told the guys where the information was coming from. When the game started, my school rushed out to an early lead, exploiting the weaknesses I had noticed. But the other team adjusted, and minute by minute climbed back into the game and wound up winning. Gary's son came up to me the next day and said, "Good scouting report sir."

Meanwhile, someone keyed my car. Someone threw a rock through my window at my apartment. Someone kept repeatedly knocking on my door at night and when I opened it no one was there. Eventually, the knock came when I was dressed and shod. I bolted for the door, tore it open, and raced through it. I guessed that since I was on the end of the building that they had gone around the back, so I sprinted that way. I recognized two girls from the school running ahead of me. Leaving the door open, I called one in and demanded that she call her parents. A couple of boys I had never seen before came and sat on the steps outside the whole time. They looked like trouble. One of the girls had a connection to one of the staff at the school.

There was a big meeting about it where somehow, I was the bad guy. It was completely ridiculous, and I didn't back down, but I didn't file a police report either. The school year was winding down. Shortly after this the principal called me in and said that they would not be needing a science teacher next year and my contract would not be renewed. He then said he would never advise anyone to get out of teaching but left it open to the implication that if ever he did, I'd be the one.

As the school year came to a close two interesting things happened. One was that on their own initiative the junior high kids took a vote as to who their favorite teacher was. They informed me that I got more votes than the other six staff members put together. Clearly, the principal's opinion was not shared by the whole student body. The other thing that happened was about my last athletic duty of the year. That was the "Athletic Banquet" which was really just burgers and hot dogs at the lake.

As the kids got up and spoke about their year, they were very complimentary to the adults who mentored them. One was particularly frank and said that there was a time when they thought that maybe I wasn't such a good coach but later on they realized that I was. I left soon after that, but I didn't get a mile before I broke down sobbing uncontrollably. I had to pull over behind a pile of gravel by the roadside. I could not keep the car on the road, that's how hard I was crying. All the pain and joy and frustration and exhilaration and love and hate that had been bottled up inside me came out in a torrent. I felt justified. I felt rewarded for the amount of my heart and soul that I poured into those young people. I felt like I had done everything there that I was supposed to do. Whatever test I had faced, I passed it.

Less than two years later, that school wouldn't need any teachers at all. They closed their doors and the students there went to their area public schools. One of them later told me, "When we got to public school, we were behind in math, we were behind in history, we were behind in English, and we were ahead in science."

That didn't help me make a living though. I still needed a job. The principal had waited until the very end of the year to tell me that I was not going to be re-hired, so I missed the spring period when a lot of teachers and schools "pick new teams". My certificate was moving from "Provisional" to a plain old six-year certificate, but my experience was short, and on paper, not positive.

I had one realistic shot. That was asking in August when teachers are supposed to report back for the new year. There are always teachers who decide at the last minute that they can't come back. The administrators are in a bind in this situation because teams have mostly been picked and classes start soon. They need to take the next qualified person to walk through the door.

So, at the proper time I started contacting school districts in a flurry, starting with the ones in Northwest Arkansas where I lived and working my way down from there. This was before consolidation so there were a lot of them. And I didn't get a nibble until I got to El Dorado, which was in one of the southern tier counties of the state. The inhabitants pronounce it with a long "A" sound in contrast to how the rest of the world pronounces the legendary city of gold with the same spelling. It was on the opposite end of the state, almost as far south as you could go without being in Louisiana. They told me that there was an opening in Middle School Science and that I should drive down the six-and-a-half hours for an interview immediately.

I figured that this was the door that the Good Lord wanted me to walk through because He very helpfully provided no other opportunities to cloud my thinking. So, I started down south. It was a long drive to Little Rock, but at least I was somewhat familiar with that part of the state. Once I got beyond that, it was unknown territory for me. At the time there was a paper bag factory in Camden, which I passed through on the way. The smell was atrocious, and at the time I didn't know what it was. I just knew that the further south I drove the worse it smelled. If it kept getting worse, the thought occurred to me that I would turn the car around and skip the interview!

Of course, once I crossed the Ouachita River, the odor improved, but what a thrill crossing that river was. The bridge over which I crossed would soon be replaced, and I experienced first-hand why it needed replacing. The angle of the bridge was so steep it felt like I was going up a ramp to jump across the river. The metal grates shifted and rattled as my car moved across them. I felt like if I dared to look in my rear-view mirror, I would see that the grates dissolved as I passed over them. When I crossed the apex of the bridge and started downward, it was almost like a roller-coaster ride, only scarier because it seemed far more likely to fail. Whenever I went north after that, I took the long way toward Highway Seven and skipped that bridge, until the replacement was built.

Educator

I found the middle school and met the woman who would be my supervisor for the next nine years, Genevieve Fouse. She was a slight woman with large brown eyes who was "Old School" in the extreme. She had a reputation of being difficult to work for, but I liked her because you always knew where you stood, and she had principles and she stuck by them. At the time, I didn't know how rare that was becoming in public education. I didn't appreciate it enough. She had a much higher turnover rate than the other schools in the district. She ran me through the hoops to get me hired for one of the Eighth Grade Science positions. I had a cool old room with real lab tables, a big storage closet, and a whole wall full of drawers and two immense chalkboards. I came back and saw it some years later, after I had left teaching, and it seemed tiny and run-down, but at the time I was proud to claim it as my territory.

I had a position, but I didn't have a place to live yet. My family rented a moving truck and loaded my few worldly possessions in it and headed down. They were less than twenty-four hours behind me. I figured since I wasn't picky, it would be a snap finding a decent place to stay. It wasn't. You had to know somebody, unless you were really willing to slum it. I looked for a long time, and when my mom and stepdad and brother came into town, we looked together. We found nothing. We finally decided that we were starving and needed to eat and complain about our woes, so we went to a tiny Chinese restaurant on the main drag.

As we were discussing my plight the waitress overheard. She said that she knew a church that might be able to help. It was College Avenue Church of Christ, and they would be my landlord for nine years. It was just one of those things that helped me to know that this was what I was supposed to be doing at least for this point in my life. They rented me a run-down 600 square foot wood-frame house. It had great privacy because it was on a far corner of the church grounds. They only charged me $150 a month, and some of them felt bad about that. I painted the walls white over the dark brown paneling so that it looked bigger than a walk-in closet and did just fine for years until a skunk, possibly rabid, started tearing its way through the rotting floorboards in the back. It was tearing holes in the flooring and getting in. I called a friend with a twenty-two rifle and at the right time we took care of it, but everyone agreed it was time to move out of there.

They then rented me the former "youth house" which was brick and larger, though it too had its issues. Rent wasn't much more. I wound up attending that church for several years until the doctrinal differences got to be too much, but I really loved my days there and still have some wonderful friends from that time. Did I mention they got a gym sometime during my nine years there and so I was frequently called upon to run with them in basketball games? I basically spent my thirties in El Dorado. Life was good for a not-really-young-anymore but active guy.

I was relentless in teaching. I cared strongly about both the subject matter and the students. If a child was disturbing the class, I would go visit their parents in the evenings. Even kids that said, "We move all the time, you don't know where I stay" would be surprised to find me at their doorstep. The classes were majority black, but only by a small margin. I had no problem or trouble going to any neighborhood. Just like when I was in junior high myself, I wasn't really "cross-culturally connecting". I didn't connect that well with any culture, so I was just myself dealing with another human being who had their own unique way of looking at things. I wasn't in a group and I wasn't, in my head, dropping them into groups.

There were a lot of smart kids, and some motivated kids. Some of them cared, and some of them didn't. I would demand that they at least go through the motions like they cared. I figured if they practiced that hypocrisy long enough, it could become a real part of them through habit. And yet for my first year and one-half of teaching public school, I was not a good science teacher. In particular I was failing the children who were bright and motivated. My lessons were repetitive and superficial.

The reason for this was because of how score was kept at the time. Hillary Clinton, when she was First Lady of Arkansas, designed a "Basic Skills Test" program to, in her mind, bring measurable accountability to Arkansas Schools. I was later to figure out that all high-stakes testing distorts curricula and has negative effects on almost every kind of learning which is not measured. It doesn't matter whether Republicans or Democrats float the program, or how they dress it up. But this was a Democrat game, because that was what most of the state was at the time.

The "rules" were that the schools would be judged by how well the bottom 15% of their students did on the "Basic Skills Test". It wasn't a test of skills at all. It was a bunch of unconnected facts that didn't rise to the level of a "core body of knowledge". How well the top 85% on the test did was of no concern. Schools would be evaluated on how well the bottom fifteen percent performed. If more than 85% passed the Basic Skills Test, the school was OK. If less than 85% passed it, then the school needed remediation, not just the students. The students who failed the test would be pulled out of regular classes and drilled for the last month of the year and take it again.

Naturally we changed our instructional models to accommodate the rules. If the rules of football changed so that only field goals were worth points, you don't think that would change their priorities? I must have bored the clever ones to tears that first year and a half. I didn't do a lot of connections, and I didn't do systems. There wasn't much enrichment. It was all facts. Pounding and pounding with facts. It was the opposite of the way I wanted to teach, but that was my job. I tried every way I could think of to make it interesting, including inventing quiz-show and card type games, at least until Mrs. Fouse saw non-traditional learning going on and shut it down. At the end of the year, both middle schools passed the 85% hurdle. My percentage of students who passed was marginally higher than the scores of the other five eighth grade science teachers in the district, but not by a significant amount and it was a hollow victory for me.

Bill Clinton was elected President in November of my second year and was sworn in that January. The state legislature met that same month and one of their top orders of business was to jettison Hillary's stupid "Basic Skills Testing" program. It was gone. I could stop drilling them for unconnected facts and teach systems, context, and connections. I could really help them to train their minds for understanding. I felt like "Hercules Unchained".

I might not have gotten it all right by the end of that school year, but I was ready, willing, and able to re-design everything I had been doing and make it more like I wanted it done. There would still be a core body of knowledge, but in context, and with systems. Knowledge of facts would be the foundation of understanding, not an end in itself. I often demanded more of them, but most of the students saw that I did it with good intentions and that I was willing to give more effort back to them, and intuitively they respected that.

I had some wonderful years teaching middle school. I learned as I taught. I was talking about things I loved to talk about. I made friends, and not just among the other faculty or parents. To this day some of my best friends call me "Mr. Moore". When human souls connect, it is a rare and beautiful thing. I can remember when most of my friends were older than I was. Now they are passing on, so I am doubly glad for the younger ones I picked up along life's journey.

For a while I even considered becoming an administrator. I think I got a little over half-way done with my master's degree, but the School Law course gave me something to think about. The whole legal basis of our public schools had changed over the previous decades, even if attitudes in the trenches hadn't caught up. Public school teachers were no longer considered "Agents of the Parent", but "Agents of the State." This was done to limit the power of school officials, so there was a definite upside to it, but I could see downsides as well. Basically, in my mind I was an agent of the parents of the community. I wasn't a state agent delivering a product, but a participant in helping their child become better. It was an outmoded way to look at things. I also put a lot of heart into my work and it would really bother me when parents would fail their kids, or when kids would fail themselves. Basically, I wasn't cut out to be a Public-School Administrator. My thinking about how things should be was at odds with the times.

Heck, for the long term I was to find out I wasn't even cut out to be a public-school teacher. One needs more emotional detachment to make it a career-long thing. You can't let every setback get to you, even if some of those setbacks are students who screw up their lives before they even really get started. Mrs. Fouse called me "an angry young man" because I was always objecting to one thing or another. Truth was, I wasn't all that young anymore.

I went to Northwest Arkansas some summers. One of them I practically raised a three-year-old nephew when the other caregivers were sick or had to work. It wasn't just teaching, it was parenting. Or at least it was the closest thing to parenting I had had and it got me thinking seriously about having my own family. The trouble was, I came home from teaching emotionally and physically exhausted. By the end of the day, I had said all the words that I wanted to say. Only in the summers did I get some space. I didn't know it yet, but I was starting to transition out of teaching.

One of those summers my sister Dana helped me do a Public Access Television show where I pontificated on political issues. If I saw a tape now, I might see myself as a joke. My specialty was saying something that seemed controversial but then presenting it in a way so that many people would think it wasn't such a bad way of looking at things after all. I had fun and got my first taste of media production.

At this point I was a "Republican leaning" voter, but to the right, not the left. I never bought into the "fear button" tactics that the two parties both play on their more captive voters. If the Republicans didn't run a candidate that met my minimum standards, I didn't vote for them. For example, in 1996 Republican Presidential candidate Bob Dole was asked in a debate about his party's platform plank on abortion. He said that he hadn't read it and felt no obligation to follow it. I had followed the story about how hard the grassroots folks had worked to keep that plank. They were so happy when it was left in.

Now he was saying it didn't matter a bit.

I thought to myself, "I don't know who he is listening to, but it isn't the people at the grassroots that worked so hard to get him there." No matter how one felt on the issue, I thought it was callous and raised a red flag for me. It taught me an early lesson about party platforms and how they don't matter unless the people who are really running the show want them to matter. Some planks are just there so that voters who want to kid themselves into believing that a particular party will make a difference on the issue have a straw to grasp. The more I looked into his record, the less I saw to agree with. Dole was a big spender too. I think I voted third-party for President for the first time. I believe I voted for the candidate of the U.S. Taxpayer's Party.

Chapter Six

Registered Republican

I was later told that complaining about things, including on a tiny public access cable show, wasn't going to change anything. Instead, the way to really change things was to join one of the two political parties at the local level. I had been politically aware for a few years now, even to the extent of playing a major role in my friend's campaign for Circuit Judge, but I had no idea how to officially access the system. Apparently, that started by formally joining one of the two major political party's "County Committee" and attending their meetings.

Well, there was a time in Arkansas when there would not have been much of a point to that. The Democrat "Good Ole Boy" network ran most of the state. But the emergence of Mike Huckabee started to change Arkansas politics on the state level in the same way that Ronald Reagan changed it on the national level. It made voting Republican socially acceptable. If I am honest, Mike Huckabee had a big role in motivating me to getting formally involved in politics as well. Most people in my circles considered him a hero back in those days.

Mike Huckabee was a Baptist preacher who took to secular politics. When Bill Clinton was elected President, the Lt. Governor, Jim Guy Tucker, moved up to the Governor's mansion. To fill Tucker's old slot, there was a special election for Lt. Governor. Mike Huckabee ran in that special election. With the help of the newly energized church folks, he narrowly won. With the exception of Frank White's surprise upset of Bill Clinton, which was reversed two years later, Huckabee was the first Republican to win any statewide Arkansas Constitutional Office in over twenty years.

The Arkansas Democrats did not take this encroachment on what they considered their own turf gracefully. Huckabee reportedly arrived at the state capitol to find that they had nailed shut the door to his office from the inside, cleaned out almost all his office furniture, and had spent virtually all of his budget. I think it took about two months of public outrage before he could finally get access to his own office space. The pettiness against him only galvanized people like me to get behind him more. His motto was "unplug the machine", and the machine was showing just why it needed to be unplugged.

On paper, the Lt. Governor's office could have been an important job, because the Lt. Governor was the President of the Senate. It never mattered when The Club ran things, because they operated as a unit. I believe at this time that the State Senate started changing their rules so that the *President Pro Tem*, one of their own members they elected to really perform the job of Senate President, took over the day-to-day operations of the senate such as deciding which bill went to which committees. I believe they funded more staff for them as well, leaving the Lt. Governor's staff, small though it was, with little to do.

It didn't matter in the broad scheme of things. For the next couple of years, Mike Huckabee completely vexed the Democrat Governor, Jim Guy Tucker. Tucker called a special election to propose a state constitutional convention. Huckabee opposed it. It was voted down by a ridiculous 80-20 margin. Tucker then called for a special election on two questions in order to raise money for highways- one a proposal to raise fuel taxes and the other a proposal to issue bonds. Huckabee came out against the plan. Both questions failed by an even larger margin than the constitutional convention proposal. Huckabee also opposed Tucker's plan for school district consolidation. Many of the rural communities in the state really loved their schools. Huckabee scored more easy political points even in Democratic strongholds by opposing the plan. The Democrats seemed absolutely tone-deaf and out of touch. Mike Huckabee could do no wrong. He had the aura of a People's Champion.

Huckabee prepared to run for U.S. Senate, stirring the Democrats to a frenzy. Then fate took a turn. Jim Guy Tucker was convicted for fraud as part of the famous "Whitewater" investigation. Our state constitution prohibited convicted felons from holding such office. He agreed to step down from the Governor's office by July 15th. As Lt. Governor, Mike Huckabee would succeed him. Huckabee made the decision not to file for the U.S. Senate and the filing period closed.

At that point, Tucker announced that his case was strong, and he was considering staying in office and fighting the charges. Normal people were outraged. I was outraged. I tell you that if at that point Mike Huckabee had called for people to get their guns and come to Little Rock to force Tucker out, I would have gotten my gun and driven to Little Rock. That's how behind Mike Huckabee I was at the time.

As it turned out Tucker soon reversed himself and resigned, leaving Huckabee as Governor. It occurred to me that what just happened should have not gotten as far as it did. And the reason that it went as far as it did was that people like me were just living our own lives and not pitching in to keep things from getting that corrupt and crazy. If I was willing to pick up a rifle and fight over politics, I surely should be willing to give up a few evenings to join a political party and try and see that it never comes to that. It was time for me to "be the grown up" and get involved in the nitty-gritty of the duties of a citizen in a self-governing republic. So, at age thirty-five for the first time in my life, I became a registered Republican.

I can't remember how I found out about the Union County Republican Committee Meetings, but this was before the state went Red, so they were looking for people to join. My recollection is at the time the location of the Democrat County Committee meetings was somewhat of a secret. After all, they were the club that mattered. But this was about to change. At any rate, I showed up at a Republican County Committee meeting one night and paid my $25 dollars to join. I barely introduced myself.

It turned out that I had showed up in the middle of a big fight between two factions. That is, it was a "big fight" in terms of intensity, not in numbers. The Committee had about 25-30 members. As small as that sounds, I believe it was the largest in the state at the time, outside of Northwest Arkansas and Pulaski County. There was some old Oil and Gas money in those parts. The oil boom in Union County had died down a long time ago, and the population of the city of El Dorado was half the size that it was in the 1950s, but the oil business was still an important part of the community. Some of the biggest Republican donors in the state were from Union County, not that they ever showed up at the meetings, or even officially joined the committee. Big Donors didn't need to. They had direct ace$$ to the politicians.

The fact that the County Committee was so small should raise a red flag for you. In later years, after the Republican party became relevant state-wide, I would come to visit many Republican County Committee meetings in various parts of the state of Arkansas. There are not that many folks at any of them. I imagine it is the same with the Democrats. Even today, I wonder if the total attendance at all monthly "County Committee Meetings" of either major party in the whole state averages anywhere near 2,000 people? Frankly, I doubt it, even though they run the state now. The true number of active members isn't that great. Certainly not enough to justify the stranglehold they have over managing our political choices.

At any rate, since neither side of this new club I had just joined trusted each other, they were looking for someone who wasn't in either faction to run the thing. I walked right into a "situation". One fellow suggested that I run for Chairman. The election would be held at the next meeting, which would be my second meeting. I demurred. He said that the other fellow who was thinking of running was a "liberal" Republican who taught at the local community college and that I would be the more conservative choice. At this time, it wasn't obvious that the system had twisted and denuded those words of any stable meaning. I still demurred. I thought I wanted to be a "playa" but not even I was egotistical enough to think that I should just walk in for my second meeting and announce that I was ready to lead the group! Many of these were older folks, and I was in my mid-thirties.

Once I got the signal that they really did want me to run for a party office, I ran for and got elected to Vice-Chairman. The Professor was the Chairman. I wanted to be a "team player" and the two of us worked well together in spite of our different views. At least for a while.

Soon after, a fellow from Northwest Arkansas who I will call "Buck", persuaded me to join a para-party organization called the "Young Republicans". They are still around, I think. I was kind of old to be a "Young Republican" but I liked him, and we agreed on ideology. I was living like a guy in his mid-twenties, even if I was older. Even though it was state-wide, it wasn't very big either and I quickly wound up the Communications Director for the group.

I am just going to skip ahead to the part of the story about my relationship with Buck. He was an easy guy to like and I liked him.

I thought at one time we had the potential to be brothers of a sort. Since I spent summers in Northwest Arkansas, I visited him on occasion and got to know his wife Jenny too. We never did quite get the Young Republicans of Arkansas "legit" in our time there, but he was able to use it as a springboard to become a state legislator.

He loved the job, but during his first term he and Jenny got divorced and for one reason or another he decided not to run for another term. He asked me, and others, for advice when he was considering divorcing his wife. They had a daughter. I personally thought he was losing his grip on what was important, and I advised him not to do it.

Afterward, we kind of drifted apart. Many years later, I moved back to Northwest Arkansas and ran for the state legislature as an independent. It just so happened the district now included Buck's old home. His ex-wife Jenny still lived there, along with her new husband. I figured this out when I was going door-to-door campaigning. She remembered me and said, "When Buck floated the idea of divorcing me to all of his political friends the rest of them said "sure, do what you feel." You were the only one who said, "Don't do it, there will be consequences." Then she told me, "You have my vote and you can put your big sign in my yard."

But I am getting ahead of myself. Early on in my tenure as Vice-Chairman of the Union County Republican Committee, Governor Huckabee came to town and spoke at the local Community College. Our local State Senator, a Democrat legend named Jodie Mahony, was there speaking too. During the event Mahony was incredibly rude to Governor Huckabee. Huckabee did pretty well at trying to laugh it off, but it was forced. I remember thinking to myself, "Somebody needs to run against this guy." And of course, as an officer of the local Republican County Committee, I was in position to help see that it happened. Or so I thought.

The Mahony family was one of the most patrician families in the area and he had served as a legislator in one chamber or another for a long time. His family were all lawyers and had practiced law in the area since 1896. He was old money so he could self-finance his campaign, but he wouldn't have to because his party backed him. Heck, that would probably not be necessary because he could win big without campaigning at all. Basically, you would have to find somebody to run against him who was willing to take a beating just to make a point that the Republicans were going to provide a serious choice to the voters and the Democrats could no longer act like some kind of permanent ruling class.

It would take a miracle to upend him. I didn't have the nerve to ask anyone to put their lives on hold for months and fight like heck in order to take a beating from this guy. And no one was stepping up and volunteering either. So, in line with the excess testosterone which contributed to so much of my thinking in those days, I decided I would run against him myself.

I noticed that while the good Senator affected a down-home persona of a conservative "Blue Dog" Democrat in his district, his voting record was that of a hard-left Democrat. Of course, most people vote by feeling tone, group identity, and personal connections rather than positions on issues, but I was too dumb to realize it at the time.

Soon after this I got a call from our County Chairman. He said that a group of influential men were going to meet at probably the fanciest office in town, in a building owned by a huge Republican donor. He couldn't make the meeting and he asked if I would go represent the Committee. The purpose of the meeting was to discuss offices they thought Republicans could win and find candidates to run for them. I agreed to pinch-hit for him at the meeting, but I was taken aback by the call. Finding candidates to run as Republicans? Wasn't that our job? And whoever these guys were, they scheduled the meeting without even taking the schedule of the County Chairman into account. It was like they decided to include him as an afterthought.

I entered the conference room at the pinnacle of this tall building. A very high official of the Republican party of Arkansas was there. So was the Huge Donor who controlled the place. There were seven or eight other men in the room as well. None of them attended the County Committee meetings. One of them was the campaign manager for the State Representative from El Dorado. Funny thing was, the State Representative was a Democrat. Yet here he was, one of about ten guys there to decide who they should pursue to recruit as Republican candidates in this area.

Things went fine for a while, with the Republican Official pointing to offices they wanted to find candidates for, and names being tossed around. Finally, they came to the office of State Senator, held by Jodie Mahony. The official acknowledged that it would be a tough one, but they wanted to find a candidate to run against him.

I interrupted the dead silence that followed by saying that perhaps I should leave the room, since I was considering running against him, and had already raised $500 towards it. I didn't mention it at the meeting, but there was a tax-credit law in effect where someone could donate to a state candidate and get a $50 per person tax credit. I didn't mind asking people for money even for a long shot if they were going to get it all back in a tax refund.

The Republican Official and a couple of others asked me to pitch myself to them and describe why I thought I was the candidate to back against Mahony. I pointed out his true record on taxes, and how he sold himself as a conservative, but his record was that of a tax-and-spender. As a teacher, I was in position to poke holes in his resume on education- an area in which he was considered an expert. Not only did he have to take responsibility for implementing Hillary's "Basic Skills" program, but he was taking away local control of schools by mandating things that once were optional. The heads in the room were nodding up and down. I was moving the room.

Then I said, "And he was also one of only four state senators to vote against banning partial-birth-abortion."

The temperature in the room dropped faster than a stone. It was shocking how quickly their attitudes changed. Some of them went a shade paler, others perhaps a shade redder. I saw many knuckles tightening. "You can't talk about that!" they said. This wasn't even abortion generally that he had voted to protect, but a particularly gruesome subset used on babies that were near term called "Partial Birth Abortion".

They were unmoved by my citing polls about how voters felt about this procedure. The High Republican Official offered that he was "conceptually pro-life", whatever the heck that meant. The consensus of the room was that candidates should say that they are pro-life and then not say anything more about it. This was back in the late 1990s, when the Republican Party was publicly holding itself out as the Defenders of the Unborn. I was the only truly pro-life person in the room of men who were supposed to pick the candidates, and I was there by accident.

The conversation came to a standstill with things possibly derailed by my sincere views on the issue. Finally, the Huge Donor who controlled the building spoke up for me. He said if we focus on the education issue maybe a teacher like me would be the right person to run against Mahony. I had several dealings with him after that and politically I can truly say we never saw eye-to-eye, but he came through for me that time, if luring me into a thrashing was indeed a favor.

Fact is, I taught his kids, and I poured myself into them as I did with so many of my students. My affection for them was genuine and I believe reciprocated. I call him "Huge Donor" because that is who he was to the others. He was the father of those kids to me. That may have helped me get a pass from him, and once he spoke all the other heads started going up and down again. No one else was going to pay good money to file against Mahony, so I was "in".

Once the filing period was over the High Republican Official came back to town. The purpose was to interview the nominees one-on-one and gauge how things were going. This time he had in tow a State Senator, one of the few the Republicans had, who was considered an 'up and comer'. The guy was incredibly smooth. I entered the room and we all shook hands. I had barely sat down when this Senator said to me, "let's talk about problems, you're pro-life." Remember this was when the GOP was harvesting all kinds of votes, money, and grassroots energy, for being the pro-life party.

At that first meeting I had been stupefied by their negative reaction to the Life issue, this time I was ready. "I am", I said, "and I would describe my position on the issue as 'inflexible' so we might as well talk about something that we agree on." I was sending a message that I wasn't budging, but he at least pretended that what I was doing was "playing the game" of "just saying you are pro-life and don't say anything more about it." The rest of the meeting superficially went OK, but let's just say that I didn't get much help from the party. Heck I didn't even get my filing fee back until days before the election. I doubt that would have even happened except for what happened a little later.

I had a private meeting with the Huge Donor who spoke up for me in the meeting. He basically didn't want to back a candidate who made an issue of Mahony's support for partial-birth abortion. It didn't matter that I would vote against taxes that soaked the rich, guys like him were used to having it all their own way. Deals where conservative grassroots team up with big donors and each get some of what they want may have even been considered an insult. And among the big donors, I'd have to say that he was one of the good guys, if not the very best of the bunch. That is why I sought out a meeting with him, and not some others. He was genuinely civic-minded, generous, and had that "life of the mind" that I value. But he was used to getting what he wanted and maybe not so used to a true give-and-take discussion from politicians or political wannabes.

I think the SOP of the real pros was to tell him what he wanted to hear.

I have a perfect example of that. Governor Huckabee was also supposed to be a big pro-life supporter. How come the Huge Donor got on so well with him? I basically asked him that at our meeting. He assured me that he and Huckabee had talked about abortion, and then he made some sort of vague defense of the issue as if to say that Huckabee had been satisfied with that. So, I asked him, since Huckabee had talked to him about it, what was his reply when Huckabee told him "X".

I forget what his vague defense was but there was an easy and strong pro-life response to the argument, which I am calling "X". Any serious pro-life candidate would have been familiar with it. Fill in the blank with that response. He didn't like that, but by his reaction I surmised that Huckabee had never called him on it. He never answered with "X". Maybe the Governor had just taken the guy's money and acted like the flimsiest justification was something he'd not thought of before!

Of course, I had first gotten the idea to enter the State Senate race because I was offended at the way Governor Huckabee had been treated by the incumbent. But cracks were starting to appear on the feet of my political idol. Another one showed up when the Republican legislative candidates went to Little Rock for the purpose of meeting him and having our picture taken with him. I was among them.

First his Chief of Staff came in the room and told us that he cared more about his re-election, and less about our election. I had no problem with that. I appreciated the blunt talk, and I knew it was true anyway. What I didn't appreciate is that they had all the candidates lined up like cattle to get our picture taken with him in front of a background that was especially constructed to be, in my mind, as ugly as possible. It was a garish yellow, and some of it was shiny, with a busy pattern over it. I didn't even use it in my literature. It was that abominable.

I suppose that by going through this ritual they could say that they gave every Republican legislative candidate an opportunity to have their picture taken with the Governor, and then the ones they really wanted to win could have their picture taken with the Governor later in order to obtain one that was more usable. I noticed later that some candidates had a good picture taken with the Governor that appeared on their campaign literature. I figure that they paid for it somehow, with blood or treasure.

But that was small potatoes compared to what happened the next time Huckabee came to town. It happened to coincide with a rare visit from my half-sister, Monica, who was Essie's daughter with my father. I took her to the event excited for a chance to shake the Governor's hand and more meaningfully for me, have my sister see it. At some point after the last trip, Huckabee and Mahony must have kissed and made up, because the Governor talked to Mahony plenty that afternoon, but he wouldn't let me anywhere near him.

I mean that literally. This was before Huckabee found out about keto diets and he was a big guy. He moved with astounding agility for a man his size, constantly turning on a dime to avoid me and effectively using clusters of people to cut off my approach. I tried many times, an embarrassing number of times, to approach him and every time he would radically change course and get some people between me and him. I could either plow through a crowd and tackle him, resulting in my arrest by security, or I could just go home. I went home, embarrassed. I figure they got a big laugh out of it.

I quickly realized that I was on my own, but the actual campaign was going well. I just focused on talking to voters in the district and not politicos. I discussed the Senator's full record, including abortion. Sometimes people would try to tell me "he's a conservative Democrat", and I just went down the list of taxes, centralization of control of education, and the partial birth abortion vote. "What part of any of that is conservative?" It was a true stumper.

The east side of El Dorado was old-money and issues didn't matter at all. Being upper-class vs. barely middle-class was what mattered and I quickly learned to focus on the west side or go to the rural areas to campaign. I even spent some time in the African-American neighborhoods. I was a teacher who in my free time played pick-up basketball and usually was the only white guy on the court, so I had more inroads than was typical. I don't think I swung a lot of votes, but even a few percent gain was basically doubling the usual GOP vote in that community.

The Republican County Committee put a car in the Martin Luther King Jr. parade with a big sign "Party of Abraham Lincoln" on it. They put me in the back seat with our only black member, a local pastor. He was shocked at how many in the crowd were calling out my name and waving to me.

Even fund-raising was going miraculously well. Someone gave me a heads up that a small businessman might be interested in giving money to my campaign. I called him up and he said, "Let's talk today." My car was in the shop, but I bicycled over the three miles or so in my faded blue jeans, sneakers, and t-shirt. We talked for a while and really hit it off. I was sympathetic to all his concerns, which didn't happen very often. After about twenty minutes he said that he was going to raise $5,000 for me, which was a huge chunk of what I raised. I think he gave me $2,000 on the spot and later other checks came in from his family for the rest. I bicycled back home stunned at the turn of events.

Between that and the small donors I had money for small and larger yard signs, stakes, radio-spots, a push-card, and a mail-out for most of the county and parts of one or two others. People were really volunteering to take my signs too. The west side in particular had major streets that just showed one bright red Moore sign after another for as far as the eye could see. My radio spots hit him pretty hard, especially as his radio spots featured his role as a "tax cutter". In my ad I said that "he was talking about what a big tax cutter he was, and while I like a joke as much as the next person, you deserve to know the real story....". I then laid out his actual record of taxing anything that moved.

The subject of debates came up and some organizers asked me for my input. I said, "How about two a week from now till the election?" They demurred on that, but we agreed on some reasonable terms for a first debate. Even though I was a teacher, I was no longer a member of the Arkansas Education Association for plenty of good reasons I won't get into here. Of course, they endorsed Mahony as he had a huge reputation as an education expert.

I had examined his bills in detail and wasn't nearly so impressed. The AEA representative was a friend of mine, but it was his duty to announce in the teachers meeting that if anyone wanted to come out and support Mahoney in the debate against me that they should make every opportunity to come. I stood up and said if there was anyone there who wanted to watch me kick Mahony's tail they should also come. They could also listen on the radio. A little tension there.

I showed up at the amphitheater early and observed the debate just previous to mine. There were two podiums. The one assigned to the Democrat was well-lit. The lighting on the other podium was atrocious. The Republican was lit like a character from a horror movie. As soon as that debate was over, I headed up to the well-lit podium and dropped my notebook on the podium and did not budge. To ask me to move would have been suspicious.

There was an issue though when the moderator of the debate, who I will call James, came up a few minutes prior to the debate and informed me that there would be no discussion of social issues permitted at the debate and all of my answers had to be pertinent to the question asked. It was clear that James did not want me talking about the Senator's record on partial birth abortion. This was odd, because among his many other civic roles, James was a board member of Arkansas Right to Life! I told James that the terms of the debate had been agreed to, and that wasn't one of the conditions. He insisted that I should limit my comments to non-social issues, and I told him I would answer how I thought best and if he didn't like it then we could just argue about it live on the radio.

I honestly can't remember if I ever mentioned it or not, I think I did once in passing. I do remember that the Senator tagged James in once, asking him to rule my comments as out-of-order for not being related to the question. In that case I was able to explain why my comments were related to the question and probably scored another point off it. After that, the Senator took his beating like a man. On education, he started by saying he favored local control of schools and went on from there. On my rebuttal I gave one example after another of his bills where he changed the law from a school district "may" do something to they "shall" do something.

The audience was also salted with a few of my bolder former students who didn't mind applauding aggressively when I gave a good line. With their help, I dominated in applause lines. He also messed up when he suggested that I didn't have proper experience for the job because I had been "cloistered in the classroom" for so much of my professional life. The teachers in the audience brought in to support him didn't applaud that line, to put it mildly. I had fun afterward with my fellow teachers who supported him by asking them how it felt voting for a guy who obviously thought so little of what we do!

Skipping ahead a bit, after the election I asked James how he, as a board member of Arkansas Right to Life, could endorse Mahony and do all the things that he did for him. To his credit, James came clean. He said that Mahony promised him that if James came over to his side, he would sponsor a strong pro-life bill. Naturally, when the time came the language in his "pro-life" bill was so full of weasel-words and mile-wide loopholes that even Arkansas Right to Life came out against the bill, decrying it for the obvious fraud that it was. After that James and I developed a friendship and respect. He later asked me to be on the state board of Arkansas Right to Life, but I demurred. I had been asking people for favors and had no way of returning those favors. My friends were poor or middle-class. I knew I could not raise money for them the way they would need a board member to and thought the slot should go to someone in a better position to help the cause, not polish my resume.

I guess word got back to Republican headquarters in Little Rock and maybe the Governor that this Moore guy was really putting up a fight and maybe they should not have brushed me off the way they had up to this point. A lady from HQ called me up and said she wanted to drive down from Little Rock and visit with me. I said she could meet me after school.

When she asked for directions, I made sure to tell her to take the roads that I knew had a massive stream of "Moore" signs. If you just judged by the "Sign Wars" along the route I gave her you would think that I was going to win by a landslide. By the time she got there she was very apologetic about the lack of support and said that the Governor was on the ballot too and he was trying to focus on his own election so that he could continue to help the whole state and so-forth. I told her that I understood, and it was OK. I don't think I mentioned to her that the reason I thought it was OK was that if by some miracle I got elected I wouldn't owe him a blessed thing! I'd only owe the people of the district, and that was my preference.

The state GOP finally did send me some money that may have been as much or more than the filing fee I paid them to enter the race, but it showed up like three days before the election when it was too late to use it effectively. Before that someone, I don't know if it was from the party or not, also did some opposition research and gave me what they claimed was personal dirt on the Senator. I had no idea if it was true and I didn't use it, even in private. Hey, the guy supported partial-birth abortion. Whatever personal foibles he may or may not have had didn't say as much as his votes said within the context of a political campaign. I wanted to keep it on the policy issues, all of them, and not engage in personal destruction. There were a few people who noticed and appreciated that on the other side, not that they said so until their guy had won!

The blooms had fallen off my Mike Huckabee roses. I also got word that Huckabee or his people had been yelling at a State Senator from Fort Smith who I really liked, a dignified lady about my mother's age name Peggie Jeffries. Some of my friends told me that she had been moved to tears by the threats and verbal abuse she endured for failing to cooperate in his move to what I then called the left, all the while spewing good ole' boy conservative rhetoric. The idea of her being so treated riled me, to say the least.

You remember how his star rose by opposing more highway debt and tax proposals and school consolidation from his predecessor Jim Guy Tucker? He would then turn around and support all those things once he got in the Big Chair. I thought of it as the "left" then, but it was really just corporate cronyism and centralizing as much power as possible. I now realize that both major parties do it, they just dress it up with left or right rhetoric to fool the people who support them. The right used to have a harder job of doing that because debt and taxes didn't fit with a traditional conservative vision. By now I think rank-and-file Republicans have been worn down by their profligate leadership to the point where Stockholm Syndrome has kicked in and they are not offended by the growth of government like they once were.

As it turned out, I only got 38% of the vote. He won the patrician east side of El Dorado, which was by far the biggest city in the district. He also did well in the black neighborhoods. I won the west side. I didn't have the reach to get to the rural parts of the other counties that were in the district, so he won there too. But when it came to the rural areas of Union County, I did quite well. In fact, on election night we were both on the radio when the results started to come in, beginning with the rural precincts in our county. I won five of the first twelve boxes reported. When it was his turn to be interviewed, he described the results to that point as "humbling".

The results looked a lot better on a map of the county. In terms of area, I won half the county, maybe more. To prepare for the next Republican County Committee meeting, I took a county map and used yellow highlighter to show the precincts where I won. Relations between the Chairman and I were eroding a bit, as he was failing to charm me into jettisoning any of my views regarding the size and scope of government, or social issues. When it was my turn to give the "after action report" on my campaign he instructed me in front of the others not to talk too much, maybe two minutes at most. One of the members later commented to me about how rude he was about it.

It didn't matter. I had a picture, which is worth one thousand words, so I said "I will only need one minute, Mr. Chairman. Here on this map in yellow are the precincts where your Republican candidate beat Jodie Mahony." I then dramatically unfurled the map. There was an audible gasp in the room as the mostly El Dorado East side folks were shocked to see how strongly I had done away from where they lived.

The Chairman was too clever to ever directly engage me in policy discussions. Instead, he would set up situations where we were supposed to listen while someone else told us how it should be. The party has fundraisers called "Lincoln Day Dinners" where the speaker is supposed to get up and make a few self-deprecating jokes, give some rah-rah stuff to the troops, and sit down after about twenty minutes. Instead, he brought in the Party Chairman of the first Congressional District on the eastern part of the state. The guy harangued us for about two hours on the subject of how "right-wingers are screwing up the party." His profanity-laden speech was more lashing out at his own grassroots than any party building. I lost my cool and walked out on him, which was regrettable only because I had a few young friends I had invited who didn't want or deserve that kind of attention.

Afterward some of the committee said, "The District Chairman wants to talk to you." I said, "He's talked to me plenty, and I've listened to him plenty. If we meet, it is so I can talk to him and he can listen." There was no meeting.

My activism took another turn when Juanita Broaddrick made what seemed to me to be credible allegations that Bill Clinton had raped her in 1991. I was offended that the despicable establishment media seemed to be sitting on the story. If someone they didn't like had been accused of the same thing, it would have been the subject of fifty-eight "Special Reports" with the "journalists" reporting in indignant tones with nostrils flaring. Instead, the few times they did cover the story the angle was something like "how will the Republicans exploit these allegations for political purposes?" Meanwhile, President Clinton was about to return to his original hometown of Hope, Arkansas for a visit where he would, no doubt, be honored.

Well, my buddy Mock was just as ornery as I was. It didn't sit well with either one of us that this was going on. You may remember when Paula Jones made an allegation against Clinton his flying monkeys went on TV and insinuated that she was trailer trash out for money. Broaddrick was a professional woman so basically that lie wouldn't fly and they had to downplay the story. Mock and I decided that even if we couldn't force them to be honest, we could make being crooked more uncomfortable for them.

I printed up a bunch of posters with Bill Clinton's picture on it. It was a frame from when he was wagging his finger at us claiming that he "did not have sexual relations" with Monica Lewinsky. The caption over the picture said something like "WARNING: ACCUSED SEXUAL PREDATOR IN YOUR AREA". They were modeled on those posters from "Megan's Law" where you had to warn people if a sexual predator was coming to live in their neighborhood. Beneath the picture the posters said that there were well-corroborated allegations that this man had raped a woman named Juanita Broaddrick.

Mock and I drove to Hope that night and we put those posters up anywhere Clinton or the media were likely to be the next morning. And then we went to the park and any other prominent public place we could find and put them up there as well. It was a good time for a good cause.

Earlier I mentioned maps. As a part of my campaign plan, I had taken city and county maps and drawn in the lines for every precinct. I had obtained this information from the County Clerk's office. I just walked up to the counter and asked for the maps with the precinct lines. All county offices were controlled by Democrats. They readily provided them to a nice-looking clean-cut white man. I copied the lines right there in their office on my maps and that was it.

Later, I happened to be in the County Clerk's office on other business when a black guy I knew from playing pick-basketball came in. His name was Billy. We exchanged greetings. He then walked up to the desk and asked for the same information I had asked for a few months before regarding precinct lines. "I am sorry, we don't provide that information.", said the attendant behind the desk. Of course, they had provided it to me previously.

I pulled Billy aside and explained to him that I had the same information he was asking for at my house. I am not even sure I pulled him very far aside. I didn't care if the attendant heard me. I was offended that she was pretending they didn't give that out to one color constituent, but readily provided it to someone of the "right" color. And this from the office of a public official whose party enjoyed over 90% of the black vote!

It turned out that Billy was working for the local NAACP, that is who had tasked him with getting the precinct lines. That night,

Billy and another gentleman from the NAACP came by my house and handed me some blank maps. I copied the lines I had on my maps onto theirs while they watched, and that was it. This was in preparation for the 2000 election cycle I think, the last one in which those lines would be any good because redistricting would apply to the next cycle.

At that point, I was getting fed up with the Republican Party in general and that of Arkansas in particular. It occurred to me that I may not be the right person to represent these folks, as I saw the world kind of differently. I now think that is not a deal killer, but you must have other traits to go along with it that I had not developed. Nevertheless, when the 2000 election cycle came around, I was approached about running for what was now an open seat in the state House. The district was basically El Dorado and nearby rural areas, all within Union County.

Unlike last time, when it was just me thinking that I should run, other people were telling me that I should run. Some were from the east side of town and some from the west side. One of them, Clark, was a professional man about my age. I taught his children. He was the kind of man I thought that I wanted to be closer friends with. He had a winning personality and was highly competent. When we went around town together people thought we might have been brothers. At the time, I felt like he could have been. He volunteered to manage my campaign and he was good at it. Between him and others, including a prominent family from the east side who also said they would back me, I was persuaded to jump into the race.

The situation in this race was the polar opposite of the State Senate race. There, no one wanted to take a beating for the good of the party. This was an open seat and the Republicans might have had a chance to win it. This time securing the party nomination could be a major obstacle. I was told that I had to look strong in order to scare off other potential challengers from entering the primary. They were especially concerned with a Doctor I'll call

"Fuller", from the east side. Whether his resume was impressive or awful depended on how you looked at it. On the one hand, he was a wealthy man who was both a doctor and a General in an Air Force Reserves medical unit. He had been in the Republican Party a long time and back in the day had even run for Lt. Governor. He had married into the upper crust and lived in a mansion.

On the other hand, that marriage hadn't worked out. Even though he was rich, he had declared bankruptcy and defaulted on his creditors, some said in a most pernicious manner. And he had just been diagnosed with cancer, a very serious form of cancer. Even with my policy against personal attacks this small herd of pachyderms in the room could hardly be avoided. This stuff was already out there. Why he would even want to mess with this in that situation was beyond me, but that was the rumor. I needed someone big from his circle to come out and endorse me in order to dissuade him from entering the race.

I decided to go back to the Huge Donor who was at the original meeting behind closed doors and whose willingness to give me a chance then was appreciated. Even though we didn't see the world the same way, I liked him, and I thought a lot of his children. He was connected to Dr. Fuller socially but not all those connections went well. So, I asked for and got the meeting.

The meeting was pretty much a disaster. Not only were our past policy disagreements rehashed, but he had some disparaging remarks to say about a local pastor of a prominent Southern Baptist church who had inserted himself into a couple of minor moral crusades in the community. To me it was out of the blue, but the guy happened to be my pastor. I was a member of the Committee on Committees at that church. We stayed civil, but I bridled at his insinuations and told him that was my pastor.

Looking back, I will confess to you now that Huge Donor was more right about the guy than I was. But the meeting was pretty much ruined. He asked me if I had come there to ask him for money. I told him, truthfully, that he had a good name in the community and that was more valuable than money. I had come to ask him to introduce me when I announced my campaign. Of course, he declined. I never did ask him for money. I know he went along with it and got some things he thought he wanted too, but I also thought that politicians from "my" party were basically just telling him what he wanted to hear in order to keep using him as an ATM machine. They made a big show of listening, but did they really listen? I found the whole process distasteful and insincere. I always handled it differently. I answered back, but I was really listening.

Doctor-General Fuller declared for the race soon after and campaigned with maniacal focus. I hate to say that a much older man suffering from cancer outworked me, but he probably did. My only excuse was that I continued to pour myself into my students each day and would come home exhausted and out of both words and emotional energy, while he basically didn't have anything else to do but campaign. I think maybe it was his way of coping with his illness. Maybe if he could knock on more doors than me, it would help him believe for a while that he was OK, and not dying.

Running against him was completely different than running against Jodie Mahony, because he had no record in public office to run against. He was a "Country Club Republican" though, and it was obvious that I was the conservative in the race. I was fine with running on who I was and what I believed.

I had fun running radio spots talking about how I was a "right-wing, tax-cutting, gun-toting, conservative Republican". One of my former students, Brennan O'Donohoe, was at that time a placekicker for the Arkansas Razorbacks, and he cut a commercial for me. That one also had a playful tone. I wasn't taking myself too seriously. Unfortunately, my opponent was taking it very seriously, and ran spots where someone suggested that I was a little mentally unstable. The next time I saw the political consultant wannabe who was helping him with his campaign I told him I thought those radio spots were below the belt. He advocated ruthless campaigning, he was the one who got me the dirt on Mahony that I did not use, so I thought he might have been behind them. He quickly disavowed having anything to do with it. I could tell that even he was embarrassed.

The one part of it that might have hit home was the charge that I was too conservative to represent the district or win the election. Back in those days, six weeks before the primary election most Republicans sounded like Pat Buchanan, but in my case, some people were afraid that I meant it. In south Arkansas "conservative" just meant that the people who are running things now should keep running things, no matter what their policies. My conservatism wasn't that at all- quite the opposite, I was more a fan of true free markets unhindered by the cronyism that is endemic in our times. I was a fan of merit in a political climate that favored who-you-knew.

Still, on policies like the size and scope of government, I was surely a fan of more limited government than the courthouse crowd and many others in the community. Government was a peaceful way to divide the loot to some folks, and the more loot they could get away with the better. I had to have an answer to the charge, and I did.

The natural tendency of government is to grow, to expand. Every year, it spends more than the previous year and assumes powers that it didn't have. That hasn't changed in my lifetime no matter how people have voted. It is like gravity. If you like things about where they are now, you don't need to vote for someone who intends to keep things like they are now. If you think government is about the right size now, then you need someone who intends to make deep and painful cuts in the size and scope of government just to keep things the same.

Fact is, if you elect a wild-eyed conservative cave man who wants to smash government spending with a stone ax, it doesn't mean that government goes away. It just means that he might be able to hold off the next tax increase by another two years. It takes a Maximum Effort just to stem the tide of nature, which is for government spending and control to grow like a cancer until it consumes its host society. The only way to keep it the same is to elect people who will work tirelessly to cut it more than you want them to.

Same thing on social issues really. If you don't elect people who are pro-life fanatics, then you will be rolling out of bed to go to work to earn money which will be used by the government to pay for abortion. Even partial-birth abortion on a baby very close to term. As a matter of fact, we are doing that right now. Abortion providers get many millions of taxpayer dollars each and every year. Voting for moderates doesn't produce moderate outcomes. It produces out-of-control government outcomes.

Another example: If you don't have any ill will towards homosexuals, but still don't think that people ought to be fined out of business or sent to jail because they don't want to bake a cake celebrating a homosexual union, then you shouldn't vote for people who share your position. You must vote for people who are way to the right of your position. You must vote for politicians that are hysterically denounced as "homophobes" by an outraged media just so that government policy stays in the sensible middle ground that I just described. If you want to see moderate policies, you must vote for extremely "conservative" politicians.

There are all kinds of groups with all kinds of agendas and no qualms about using government to force people to conform to their expectations of behavior. There are all kinds of groups with all kinds of ideas about how to use the government to transfer wealth from your pockets to theirs. It may be by forcing you to buy their product whether for yourself or make the taxpayer pick up the tab when others use it. Or they could engage in rigging the rules so that no one else can profitably enter their business. Whatever. There are many ways to use government to get an edge, if people are willing to be single-minded and ruthless enough. Voting is like throwing a ball across a field with a stiff wind. To hit where you want it to, you need to take into account which way the environment is going to move things and aim further to the other side from the spot you want to hit.

As with the previous campaign, there was a debate. Since it was a Republican debate I had more of a say in the rules and we put some back-and-forth into it. Someone even asked me a question about the Doctor-General's bankruptcy, but I didn't have the killer instinct and just asked everyone to use their own judgement. For the rest of it though, it was completely one-sided. Too bad almost no one makes up their mind based on how candidates do in a debate! Even the reporter that was there wrote the article on it in a way which indicated I won the debate, along with an unflattering picture of him.

Later she told me that she got some grief in the newsroom for writing that report the way she did, because her colleagues felt it should be more neutral. "You reported what actually happened." I assured her. "It would have been bad journalism to report that debate like it was even because it wasn't even. You told the truth." I haven't had a lot of occasions since that day to say words like that to a newspaper reporter!

Despite that, things were not decided by ideas, performance, or capabilities. Who was socially connected to whom mattered most to certain key demographics. The guy from the east side who encouraged me to run and said he'd back me pretty much disappeared in the last three weeks before the election.

The night of the election, I found myself back on the air at the same radio station Mahony and I had been interviewed on as results poured in. I can't help but think that someone went to some trouble to set me up to be embarrassed, as he had been in the previous campaign. Every box that they reported while I was live on the air was overwhelmingly in favor of Fuller. If that's what they were trying to do, it didn't work. I just kept saying, "Hey that's another box from the east side of town, his neighborhood. When they report results from the West Side it is going to be a different story", and "I wonder why every box they are reporting is from the same part of town?" I wanted the audience to get what was going on there. At the end of the interview I said, "Don't worry Mark Moore fans, when we hear from the West Side things will be different."

Well, they were different, but not different enough. Thank a merciful God, I lost that primary by sixty-four votes. The upper crust of the traditional Republicans wasn't really interested in an alliance with the younger more conservative professionals that made up much of the grassroots. We were the kind of people they hired to run their affairs, but not treat as social equals. Nor were they interested in any of the ideas of limiting government or moral issues. There was a divide there and there was really no way to bridge it because there was no interest in dialogue. The idea that they should even have to do that seemed to be demeaning to them.

That didn't apply to endorsements though, and Fuller wrote me a letter asking for my endorsement, as was his right. He beat me, and if one was to enjoy the advantages of party membership one should abide by the conventions of the party. And that was to endorse the person who defeated you regardless of what you thought of them. I wasn't above that rule. On the other hand, I was done with the Republican Party. I chose to resign from the Republican Party and relieve myself of any obligation I had to endorse him.

The "Democrat" candidate for the seat was a former Republican County Chairman. That's just how things worked in the Club. The real power didn't get hung up on political labels, that was just to give the grassroots a team to cheer for while what is important stays the same no matter which side the establishment coin lands on each election. He beat Fuller like a drum in November, and Fuller died not long afterward.

Chapter Seven

All Kinds of Changes

So there I was, pushing forty, frustrated in politics, frustrated with my personal life, and frustrated with teaching. I started avoiding going to church on Father's Day Sunday because I felt that at my age, I should be a married man and a father. The Bible may say something like "get married if you have to" but the church culture in America says "you have to get married." My heart goes out to those who are like I was, just different enough that finding a soulmate is difficult or maybe not even something you are obsessed about.

Unfortunately, I spent all my emotional energy on other people's kids. When I got home from work, I had said all the words I wanted to say that day. I was emotionally drained. I didn't have the knack, like the good ones that last in the profession do, of distancing myself from the personal aspect of it. When parents screwed up perfectly good kids, it bothered me. When kids made idiotic choices that could mess up their lives, it bothered me. As education policy grew increasingly moronic, it bothered me.

I had been elected by my peers to serve on the district "Advisory Committee". I thought it was where the Administration got input from the teachers. It turned out our Superintendent thought he was supposed to advise us. I told my Principal to take me off it before I opened my mouth and got fired. She did. But I was increasingly fed up with my circumstances.

Basically, I needed to make a change. I thought if I got another job the rest of the changes would take care of themselves. I had been writing some simple software to help my students learn the material and it had worked out well. With a more sophisticated programming language I could do a lot better. So, I resigned from my job and rolled the dice. I bought "Visual Basic", taught it to myself, and started writing some educational software. In my head, I was done with teaching.

I thought my software was good, but all any of the schools cared about was whether it aligned with their ever-shifting state standards. I got a couple of nibbles, but the fact is I failed to sell my product. You had to be connected enough to know what the standards were going to be and develop your product to match them by the time they were announced. It helped if the state was "recommending" your product. I wasn't connected, I just knew how to get kids to learn stuff. It didn't take long for me to figure out that I needed to go back to teaching, at least for the time being.

Fortunately, Mrs. Fouse was very willing to hire me again. The person she had hired to replace me resigned after the first quarter. I was right back in my old job again for another year. It was the same classroom and everything. That didn't provide for any of my higher-order needs on Maslow's hierarchy, but at least I could eat!

Naturally I was looking for a new political home as well. I remembered that in 1996 I had voted for the candidate for the "U.S. Taxpayer's Party", so I decided to use this new-fangled thing called the "Internet" to look them up. It turned out that they had changed their name to the "Constitution Party" and their website listed a contact in Arkansas. A man named "John Windsor".

I contacted him and he said that his business took him all over the state and that he would soon be in Union County to look up a title in the County Courthouse. We arranged to meet. He was a nice guy and we saw eye to eye on a lot of things. Joining the Constitution Party wasn't one of them! I kept saying, "I want to join, what do I do?". He kept trying to talk me into joining the John Birch Society. I said, "I don't want to join them, I want to join the Constitution Party of Arkansas." Eventually he admitted that there was no Constitution Party of Arkansas. That the handful of folks they had fell apart. He doubted that he could find more than one other person even willing to attend a meeting. It took four people to even make a board.

I hadn't really thought about doing anything in this party I had sought to join, I just wanted to be a member of a party. As usual though, nothing good was happening unless I helped make it happen. I told him to sign me up, he could be the Chairman, I could be Vice-Chairman, the other person could be Secretary and we would find someone somewhere to be Treasurer, which should be an easy enough job since we had no money and no plans to get any. He agreed to do that.

I drove to Little Rock where we held our re-launch meeting. I shook hands with the Chairman and met the other two people crazy enough to do this. Then I went home. I was willing to work to build the party, but if any job was easier than "Treasurer" of an outfit with no money it was the office of "Vice-Chairman". I was supposed to fill in for the Chairman when he couldn't perform his duties, and he seemed in no great hurry to acquire any duties! For a month or two things coasted along like that. Hey, I was willing to help but it was really the responsibility of the Chairman to lead.

Two months later, he took a job up north and moved out of the state, leaving me to fill his shoes as Chairman. Oops. By then we had another person available to fill out the board, but not much more than that. I was now responsible for building the party, so I tried to do that.

That meant going to a bunch of meetings, sometimes with folks who turned out to be fringe. I remember I and a couple of others met with this group called "Concerned Citizens". Somehow, I had missed the flap Huckabee had gotten over attending their functions before he swore off them due to concerns about racism. They played their cards close to their vest though and listened politely and asked good questions. At least until some other visitors started asking me openly racist questions.

It turned out that it was a guy I will call Rogers and a few of his posse. He became notorious later on. He was a guy who devoted most of his life to forging a stronger White Supremacy Movement. It turns out he failed to do that, probably because he was fairly smart and well-spoken and most of the folks who he aspired to lead were anti-social blockheads who didn't trust people who could speak intelligently. What a waste of one's existence, to try and do that and still fail.

The Constitution party at the time had an explicitly Christian preamble to their platform. I was fine with religious "bigotry" but had no patience for racial bigotry. At the time atheists were banned from holding public office in Arkansas and I was OK with it. I didn't want them in the Constitution Party either. I was looking for (non-racist) Christians. I figured most European countries had "Christian Democrat" parties. Later I would get a big lesson in why the Founders took a dim view of religious tests for office.

At any rate, we contended with the racists but the guys running the meeting just grinned like possums. I could not wait to get out of there, but there was another visitor there who made coming worthwhile. That is where I met Frank Gilbert. He was also disgusted with the racial turn of the proceedings and approached us after the meeting. Frank is known now as a perennial candidate for the Libertarian Party of Arkansas, but that sells him short. So far as I know he is the only man in history to serve in an elected office in Arkansas as a Republican (Coroner), Independent (Mayor of Tull) and a Libertarian (Constable). Those last two were to come later. For a while, he joined the Constitution Party, but more importantly became a lifelong friend.

Meanwhile great misfortune struck my family back in the northwest part of the state. My stepfather, who had been a rock for my mother and really all of us, suffered a heart attack and a stroke. He was confined to a wheelchair and suffered mentally as well. Meanwhile my sisters had their own troubles. It was becoming obvious that my sister's son had some kind of disability. He started regressing in speech and sociability at about eighteen months. Later he would be diagnosed with autism. She was already pregnant with her second child when we figured this out, and she too was disabled. My mother asked me to move back closer to home so that I could provide more support. My stepbrother had already moved back into the area.

I agreed to move back to Northwest Arkansas. At first, I wasn't crazy about the idea. I was doing it out of duty, but by the time I left I felt like a ghost. I was wondering what I was still doing down south. One thing was certain, I still wasn't happy with teaching. I thought that maybe a change of scenery would help. I'd get a teaching job up there and basically give it one last chance.

Remember when I described how Hillary Clinton's high stakes testing was distorting the curriculum? Well, that kind of stupid is bi-partisan. Huckabee's attempt to institute high stakes testing had its own problems. Lucky for me that at that point the tests were only in English and Math. Unfortunately for my colleagues in those fields, I believe the intent was to make tests that the kids could not pass. That would show how "deficient" the schools were and "justify" more intervention from the state.

They wanted a reason to meddle and increase control in local schools. So, they would write a test that few could pass and then use the failure to perform on their test as a reason they should have more power! When they got their way, new iterations of the test could be made progressively easier, and of course the schools would start teaching to the test. Those two things would ensure "measurable progress under our wonderful leadership" or some such rot as that. It was a game for political credit-harvesting.

For all her faults, at least Hillary Clinton wanted to hold both schools and students accountable for failure to perform. There were consequences for both. The Huckster just wanted to hold schools accountable, but not the students taking the test! If they didn't want to put out a maximum effort, then there was no consequence to them. Only the school was held accountable. Of course, that fits with what I just said about it being a set-up to justify local districts losing more power to the state.

The test, which was called "Smart Step" or something like that, went to the other extreme of Hillary Clinton's test. Whereas hers taught only facts without context or skills, this one was just about content-free. It was a measure of skills, not knowledge. It might ask you to solve a word problem, but it didn't require you to know any facts. My buddy Pes was a math teacher who was under the gun for poor scores (like everybody else). She told me, "It's not math".

I asked her what she meant. A sample problem she showed me revealed that it was really testing reading comprehension, and only secondarily mathematics. A student could have an excellent grasp of all the math required to solve the problem but still not have a clue how to solve it simply because their reading comprehension was inadequate. The math teacher would be held responsible for this inadequacy, even if the rumor that it was deliberately written with this result in mind was true. It wasn't a great time for teacher morale.

Still, teaching was what I knew and there was only so much change I could handle at once. With what was going on with my family, and my changing location, I needed to give teaching another chance. In my mind a last chance. It turned out that my stepbrother was the Head Football Coach and a history teacher in Pea Ridge, way up in Benton County. He said they had a science opening at the middle school. That person would also coach the seventh-grade football team. I told him that I wasn't certified to coach football. He said that wouldn't bother the Principal, as she wanted a coach separate from him and the others who would do their own thing. I applied for, and got, the position. I am probably the last person in Arkansas to have been a head coach of a public-school football team on any level who did not have a coaching certificate.

I say "Head Coach" because at first, I figured I would get an assistant coach. I figured wrong. The principal stuck me with thirty seventh grade boys, twenty of whom expected me to dress them in pads every day! It was chaos. At some point another staffer took pity on me and decided to help, but I saw nothing of my brother or the other coaches. There was no communication between me and the rest of them. I didn't even know when team photographs were, so we missed them and I had to take a picture of them myself.

I think that the year before that in the Pee Wee league the group I was coaching lost every game, often by blow-out margins, but somehow, we were competitive on the field. I think we were 2-5-1 and the losses were still close games. I threw myself into coaching them with my usual aggressiveness and energy. My brother did have time to show me a little of his schemes, and he was pretty much a coaching genius. Once he was named AA Coach of the Year and twice more a state All-Star coach. What interaction I had was sound stuff.

I also became a homeowner for the first time. It was almost by accident. I tried to find a rental in Pea Ridge, but the one place I could get in, the owners wanted to treat me like a child, laying down absurd restrictions on how high I could turn on the air conditioner and things like that. I was about to turn forty! Then I locked my keys in my car. While I was waiting for a locksmith, on a whim I decided to call a realtor. I didn't have a down payment, and I could not afford much but as long as I was stuck there, I decided to take a look.

A realtor came and showed me two houses. One of them was a little cedar house that had never been painted. It was really built as a guest house for the bigger home next door, but there were no other houses near it. It had woods behind it and was built on three lots. It was barely over 1,000 square feet and had one small bathroom. The rail fence was covered with barbed wire. The whole thing was a man cave. I think I paid $67,000 for it and used a GI loan and a first-time home buyer's plan to get in with zero down. It needed work, and I got to work. For the first time in my life, almost by accident because I was into ideas more than material goods, I became a property owner. It is nineteen years later and as I write this I am still living in the same house when I am not on the road.

When I moved to Northwest Arkansas, I had some money left over from my failed campaign for State Representative down in El Dorado. I needed to dispose of it in one of the ways that the law allowed. One of those ways was to donate it to other campaigns. I was in the Constitution Party now, but I had raised that money as a Republican, so I figured the right thing to do was to pass it on to good Republicans, if I could find any.

I asked my friend James who was on the board of Arkansas Right to Life, the host of that debate with Jodie Mahony, who he would give the money to. He suggested two State Representatives. One of them was a guy named Jim Bob Duggar. The other shall remain nameless for now. I gave money to both, explaining that even though I was in the Constitution Party now, I was giving the money to candidates of the party I was in when I raised it. I expected a thank-you letter. Jim Bob sent a very gracious thank-you letter. To my surprise, he also somehow got my phone number and called to thank me personally. We had a nice visit, which included me reminding him that we met before back when he was in the tow-truck business. The other fellow never responded.

Sometime after that we had enough people interested in the Constitution Party to hold a very modest "State Party Convention" in the banquet room of a local hotel. Some may remember Gary North. He attended, but he did not want to speak. Either he wasn't sure of us or this was still too soon after he was wrong on "Y2K". On a side note, I had been asked about Y2K when I was campaigning for State Representative down in El Dorado. I correctly predicted that it would be no big deal. At any rate, we needed a keynote speaker.

I called Jim Bob Duggar up and asked him about doing it. This was before his TV show. He was just a local character and state representative then. He recommended a lifelong friend of his who was now a State Senator from Springdale – Jim Holt. I did not know it at the time, but Senator Holt was trying to raise his profile because he was contemplating a run for U.S. Senate against incumbent Blanche Lincoln. Jim and I really hit it off. The convention went decently well, but really getting to know him was the highlight of the thing for me. We even got a nice write-up in the paper that had a picture of me and him in deep conversation.

It didn't take long before the Pea Ridge middle school principal and I were clashing. I admit that I was getting fed up and maybe had a chip on my shoulder by that point, but I noticed that plenty of others were feuding with her as well. She or someone took coaching duties away from me for the following year. That didn't crush me, I had enough going on in my life. She tried to fire me, but the board would not go along with it. There was a definite sense that the board did not support her. The Superintendent was resigning, and I thought I would hang around and see what the new person did.

To show you how insane the high-stakes testing was, we were told that *every* class was to teach math and English, because those were the two subjects being tested by the state. That's how "score was kept." Science was to teach math and English. Physical Education was to teach them as well. In fact, I was handed a stack of English papers to grade because the English teacher could not keep up with all the writing assignments that she was required to give in order to teach to the state test. I liked her, so I cooperated, but I was not shy sharing what I thought of the overall policy. If I had wanted to teach English, I would have pursued that. I liked science.

I wound up doing a little radio around that time. There was a man named Jay Cole who bought time on a local Christian station. He was locally famous (or perhaps infamous in some quarters) for his TV commercials featuring blunt talk about all sorts of issues, but mostly dealing with a need for repentance and seeking God. His message was very poorly received in the college town of Fayetteville, but he stuck with it for so many years that I think he gained a grudging credibility from many quarters. Even people who grated at his Christian-talk could admit that he had a point when he talked about government corruption.

Jay started having trouble breathing, and he couldn't talk for a whole show, so he kept inviting me on to co-host with him. I can't even remember how he heard about me. It was good experience though. There were even a few times that he was gone. He was paying, and I was filling in for him. When that happened, there was another guy who showed up named Jason Sheppard. He and I did the show together. I didn't know it at the time, but he would become one of my dearest friends. One of my top goals in this life is to find kindred souls. They are hard to find, and sometimes when you think you have found one it turns out to be not so, but Jason was an amazing man with a fantastic mind. Much of his genius is based on a property which I share with him- he doesn't kid himself. He sees things as they are, not as he wishes them to be.

Meanwhile things with my family continued to be difficult. My stepfather's condition was deteriorating. It was becoming clear that my sister had not one but two disabled children. Not only was it hard seeing her struggle, but in the back of my mind I wondered if I would ever find a wife, and ever have my own children. If I did, would they be at risk? Did we share some genetic issue? I helped out when I could, but boy was I wound tight. I hope I helped just by being there, but the problems were huge and made me feel small.

Work made me feel small too. The principal that I had clashed with left abruptly soon into my second year. But the turmoil was constant. In my three years there, I went through three superintendents and four principals. It wasn't just me that was fed up. In fact, by the end of my third year I was the senior certified staffer in the 7-8th grade building! Everyone else who was there when I got there had gone!

It was time for me to go too. I think everyone one of those principals wrote me up for something. I wasn't repentant on any of it. I thought it was all nonsense. Two things really brought it to a head. One was that a couple of Special Education students quit on me and I assigned them the grades they earned- an "F". I was willing to modify their work. In fact, I had done so the previous quarter. But they decided to stop working, modified or any other way.

The regional special education director and my latest principal ordered me to change the grade. I said I would only do that if the boys did the work. I was told it was illegal to do what I was doing. I said to show me that law and that I would comply with the law. She gave me a cite, but when I looked it up it didn't say anything like that. It just said I should make reasonable accommodation and I was. She said she would get a lawyer and sue me. I told her to go ahead and get one. I would get one too.

It turned out that they assigned another teacher to work with them individually, and I think that teacher basically did it for them. At any rate they turned in enough work to pass and I changed their grade. But I realized then and there that maybe the next one would not, and then I'd be out of luck. Public education was rapidly going in a direction that didn't fit my values, and I needed to leave.

Before that year ended though, something else happened. The fashion among 13-14-year-old girls at that time became very immodest. Their jeans hung down so low that half of their rear end was hanging out. They were literally showing six or eight inches of crack to the class! The Principal warned the male staff members not to correct them on it, and for once I should have listened. But when we sent them down for a check, they would just pull their britches up and it seemed like nothing was amiss. Once back in class, it was time to mess with the hormones of the boys again.

Me and my inability to keep my mouth shut, I finally wound up telling a few of them to pull their pants up because we could see their rear ends. I have a daughter about that age, and I didn't say anything to them that I would not say to her- but she wouldn't like it either. It made them uncomfortable, and they could either decide that was their fault and they needed to change their behavior, or it was my fault and I needed to change mine. Their adolescent minds decided it was my fault and they claimed "sexual harassment".

At first, I could not take it seriously. I mean, they were literally showing their rear-ends to the whole class and I was the one harassing them? I figured sexual harassment was when you tried to get people to take their clothes off, not put them on! And it was simply enforcing the school's written dress code. I took it more seriously though, when the school district kept calling people for advice until they got somebody who told them what they wanted to hear- suspend me with pay while the "investigation" was conducted. Said investigation took till the end of the school year, maybe three months.

I was furious. All kinds of feelings were raging inside me. I was figuring on resigning at the end of the year anyway, but now I wanted to be cleared of wrongdoing before I went. My friend and former pastor John Barry Baker kindly helped me with pro bono legal services. At first, he advised me just to resign without an investigation. He told me that the way the sexual harassment laws were written, there was no "reasonable cause" test. If someone felt like you harassed them in this manner, then you were guilty based on their feelings, whether a rational person would agree with them or not. It was hard for me to accept that the laws were so screwed up that they turned what should have been a good thing into a weapon to be wielded by the most reckless. Nor did I care. I told him they better come up with something because I won't resign my position until they conclude their investigation, and they didn't have just cause to can me and they knew it.

So, I may be the only person to ever be cleared of charges of sexual harassment even when there was no disagreement about what the facts were. The "investigation" was concluded, and the Superintendent signed a letter with his findings- in his opinion, no sexual harassment occurred. He advised me to write a resignation letter with a certain effective date that would maximize my pay. I went to his office. We traded letters and he apologized for the way it went down. I extended my hand and said, "thank you." We shook hands and that was it. I was no longer a teacher.

Looking back at how my life has gone since, whatever they intended, the effect was to do me a great favor. It had been increasingly obvious that I wasn't cut out for it as a career, it was just a special phase of my life that was now over. If I was inclined to hold a grudge, it would be against the adults in the situation, but I am not even going to waste any life doing that. Why should I? It was meant to be. This was the start of a lot of positive changes for me. I didn't fit in with the public-school program anymore, and that was OK.

So let me back up a bit to when I was first suspended with pay. This was maybe March. It was about that time that State Senator Jim Holt gave me a call. He was running for U.S. Senate and he wanted the help of me and the Constitution Party of Arkansas. The truth was, there wasn't much of a party, at least in terms of people willing to do some real work. We had failed to get ballot access so there would be no Constitution Party candidates. I agreed to help where I could.

When I was suspended from my job, I had to tell him. He asked very specific questions about what I was accused of and my personal habits. Once he was satisfied that there was nothing to it, he continued to accept my help in the campaign. More than that, my role got a lot bigger. The fact was that I was still drawing a paycheck all the way into July and had nothing to do. I threw myself into his campaign basically full-time. There were three of us who ran the thing. Kay took care of the financial reporting and Treasury stuff, along with some scheduling, and Jason, the fellow I met at the radio station, and I took care of the strategy and ad buys. There was also a man who was a "warrior" when it came to finding places for signs and getting them up.

Jim Holt won a crushing primary victory that May, garnering 70% of the vote in a three-way race. The grassroots made their will very clear. Many County Committees donated to the Holt Campaign. His race was at the top of the ticket in the state of Arkansas that year. You might think that the State Party would be interested in helping the top of their ticket in the state, approved by 70% of their primary voters. You'd be mistaken about that. Of course, he was up against long odds running against an incumbent Senator, so the argument could be made that a better use of resources would be to help in those races where they had the best chance to win. Remember that one, because it's going to come back up.

While there were a couple of reporters who were fair in their coverage, like Doug Thompson of Springdale, the disgusting bias and double standards of the media were a danger to the Republic, just as is the case now. This campaign was a good example of why some people call them "presstitutes" and the rest of us should, until they change their ways. Remember "Moore's Media Maxim": "The establishment media does not exist to inform the public. The establishment media exists to protect the establishment."? Well, Blanche

Lincoln was the establishment, and the people benefiting from the insider looting now feared Holt was serious with all of his "God and Country" talk of limiting government. For good reason, he was serious about it.

Again, you have to elect far-right cavemen who want to smash government spending with a stone ax just to stave off the next tax increase for another two years. If you think the government is about the right size now then you have to vote for a mad slasher who can't even say the words "government spending" without spitting on the floor, just to fight the tide and keep things about the same.

At any rate, the consensus was that Holt didn't stand a chance against Blanche Lincoln, but the media was gonna be unfair anyway, just because that's who they are. They demanded to go through every document in his life. All of them. I went over one day to find a reporter going through this huge box. It even had his report cards from high school in there! I asked what was going on and that's what he told me. They wanted to see all his records and he said he had nothing to hide.

Well, he made some bad grades in high school and those dogs printed it! Meanwhile Lincoln wasn't even living in Arkansas. Her legal address was an empty house in the Delta while her children attended school in the D.C. area where her husband also lived and worked. The NRA gave her a "D+" and they wouldn't print that either. They thought it was more important to tell people that forty-year-old Jim Holt made a "D+" in High School Algebra or something. And I think it was this campaign where the only statewide newspaper ran five editorials in six days insinuating Jim Holt was a racist because he wanted to reduce welfare benefits to illegal aliens and have a secure border. I really can't say enough bad things about the establishment media.

Arkansas has a prime location, a diverse array of natural resources, great climate, abundant water, and a hard-working population. There is no way we should be near the bottom of the barrel year after year. When a unit, any unit, underperforms for a long period of time, the reason is *always* the people who are in charge. The leadership of this state hasn't done the job of making life better for the citizens, although they seem to be doing pretty well for themselves. In Arkansas, the establishment media is largely responsible for the underperformance of Arkansas, because they have been having their way about who runs things.

The people have also been too trusting of whoever the media tells them their leaders are, maybe too focused on personalities and social connections rather than right and wrong. When people quit listening to the establishment media, put principle over tribalism, and start thinking for themselves, then we will take our rightful place as one of the most prosperous states in the union.

When July rolled around my paychecks came to an end from the district and I knew I was going to have to get a real job, as fun as it had been. I told Holt I would help out where I could, but I had to find a paying gig. My dad was great at sales and I figured that some of it had rubbed off on me. He always said, "if you are going to sell, sell something big. Selling a pair of shoes and a car or a house is the same job, but one pays more." So I found a furniture store that paid 100% commission. If you didn't produce, you didn't get paid, but if you did, you got paid pretty well for what the job was. The hours were long, and it wasn't as fun as playing political guru, but the stress was much less, and I was learning a lot.

I still helped out with that campaign through November when time allowed. I drove Jim Holt down to his debate with Lincoln. While he was a good extemporaneous speaker, and one-on-one he was terrific, he was terrible at memorizing a prepared speech- even a short one like a debate opening. His strength was "from the heart" stuff. That was a frustrating drive for us both! Somehow, he still managed to do well in the debate. Heck, he did well in the election. He was outspent 20-1 and still got 44% of the vote. Plus, turnout was huge that year, so he got the second most votes of any Republican state candidate in history. Eyebrows were raised, believe me. Some people think her weak showing made her look so vulnerable, she decided to retire six years later rather than run for another term.

Jim Holt had a lot of support from the local Republican county committees. Many of them were outraged at how little support he got from the state and national party. More than a few threatened to quit sending money into the state and national party until they agreed to start supporting Republican nominees. The party smoothed their ruffled feathers, but I guarantee you they didn't change their ways. The money that Holt supporters sent in was probably given to some smooth-talking empty suits that would "play ball" with the insiders. I could write a book just on how centralized party systems are inherently flawed and will quickly betray the grassroots very quickly but that's not this book.

The best thing that happened to me in that campaign was the people I got to meet. Holt had connections to a network of very conservative homeschool families and many of them had flexible schedules. His "body man", the political term for "Personal Assistant", that campaign was a young man named Christian Olson. I worked with him and took a liking to him. Jason had given him an old car and it was a standard transmission. I taught him how to drive it during that campaign. He too had a "life of the mind". It was intellectually enriching to be around Jason and people like that.

At the same time, Holt was very impressed with my ideas on public policy. He told the newspapers at one point that I was "the best policy guy in the country." That was a statement that he would stand by later. Not that I can make a living off of it because my skill was finding out how public policy was skimming the public and expose the scams. I could find the flaws in the system. But those flaws are usually a feature, not a bug, from those sucking off of a particular public policy. The guys that could make a living advocating for public policy tended to be paid by those doing the skimming. I wasn't going to do that.

Jim Holt introduced me to the older sister of his "body man", Christian. Melissa Olson had a beautiful smile and whole countenance really. I was not a part of this subculture I had stumbled into, but I liked some of the things that came out of it. Liking people was easy for me but trusting them was hard. I thought that these were people who put a premium on character and doing the right thing. It started to occur to me that this was the kind of people who could be trusted, to the extent any of us sinful humans can. And that was an attractive young lady.

Melissa took some time off from Children's Church at First Baptist of Little Rock and came up to Northwest Arkansas to help with the campaign. We clicked. It was more than just the superficial stuff, such as a shared love of fine tea. We shared a love of God with a skepticism of religious institutions. In her case, that included the movement her family was sort of on the fringes of.

It was started by a man named Bill Gothard. He had an outfit called "Institute for Basic Life Principles". It turned out that the Duggars were really into his teachings, and of course as his lifelong best friend Holt was too, though not so deep. Even though I liked some of the results, what little I heard of the teaching sent up all kinds of red flags for me. It was extremely works-oriented. If something went wrong, then it was because you didn't push the right buttons with God. I always considered God way bigger than that. He's never obligated to act because we are so righteous. We aren't any righteous, that's why Jesus had to pay the price for our sins. Melissa saw the same things I did. In truth, she saw it better, because she had seen it from the inside.

She had even bucked her subculture and not supported Bob Dole back in 1996, for many of the same reasons I refused to vote for him. That she figured that out so early really impressed me.

Melissa had a "life of the mind" where she wanted to know things that didn't help her immediately, just for the sake of knowing. We talked about ideas more than events or people. It turned out that her grandfather had been an engineer at the linear accelerator at Stanford University. His name was on stuff like a patent for a chemotherapy machine. Her other grandfather was a policeman who had been murdered in the line of duty. Menlo Park, California has a park named after him. It was a famous case at the time because he left a widow with four young children- including Melissa's mother Susan.

She grew up partly in California, but also spent some time in England. She was younger than me, but incredibly mature. That may have been because she had four younger brothers and even at the age of twenty-four had basically been a second mother raising them. More likely, it was just her. Some people are "born forty". Others seem to stay a teenager in their emotions all their life. She was born forty. That was handy because I was forty-two at the time.

I confessed to her young brother Christian that I intended to ask his sister out. He said that I needed to get permission from their father first! Secondly, they didn't approve of casual dating. They believed in "courting", which was just like dating in my mind, except that up front the goal is to find a spouse. It was about compatibility for marriage, not casual. Well, the fact was that I *was* looking for a spouse, so that didn't bother me. Asking her father for permission to date his 24-year-old daughter felt a little odd, especially since I was over forty, but I liked the outward purity and some of the things I saw from this subculture so I was willing to go with the flow- at least long enough to get the girl!

He gave his permission on December 15th of 2005. Our first date was to my work's Christmas party. Soon after we had a date where we walked down Dickson Street in Fayetteville, and her eyes lit up when she saw the large Used Book Store. We went in for a while and I offered to buy her a book, scoring points. She picked a Treatise on Medieval Literature by C.S. Lewis. I wasn't even interested in the subject, but I was a fan of Lewis and interested in her for being the type of person who was. I also learned more about why she was disenchanted with the teachings of Bill Gothard, but was rock solid on Christianity. Again, we agreed on the big questions. The questions that too many people never even bother to ask or think about.

Unfortunately, we lived in different cities and I rarely got back-to-back days off. It was tough to build the relationship long distance in such circumstances, but we made it work. And I was selling enough mattresses and furniture to save some money up. Maybe even enough money for a decent-looking ring and a respectable honeymoon. She was a "hot, righteous, nerd" - perfect for me. After wondering if it would ever happen for so long, I had found my soulmate. But we were still separated by hours of travel time and I was working maybe sixty hours a week. It was hard.

She wasn't the only great soul I got to spend time with on that campaign. Jason Sheppard, whom I had met when I was on the radio also turned up to volunteer in the campaign. He and I were a team. Somewhat younger than me, he looked a bit like Christopher Reeves but his attitude was more like the character "Ron Swanson" from "Parks and Recreation". He was one of those guys who was right about everything but rarely shared his views because he was also right about how few people actually want to hear truth that stands against whatever pre-existing ideas they held. Once he figured out that I really was searching for truth we had some great and deep talks. I think we both learned a lot, maybe me more than him.

Jason was an engineer by training and could basically do anything with his hands in addition to being "book smart". I once had a car with a busted power window in the back. I just couldn't get the door panel off to look at it. Jason volunteered to "help". He was easily able to get the door panel off, and quickly diagnosed the problem as a broken piece of plastic that assisted in raising the window. It was a complicated shape. I figured that was it, I was stuck with a broken window. Without pausing, Jason pulled out some tools and a block of plastic and began shaping it into what the broken part probably looked like before it busted. Then he put it all back together and the window worked.

The stereotype of staunch conservative Christians was that they had a narrow view on life. Well, he had a narrow view on truth because once you figure something out, you know every other answer to that question is wrong. That's just the way truth is. But he was very cosmopolitan in his interpersonal relations. He had friends from all over the world. That extended to his wife Wendy, who was a Chinese national from Malaysia. She was also an engineer, but she could also apply her mind to domestic arts with great success. Her quilting was at the professional level, she was better at it than almost everyone from rural America where it was part of the culture. They were just exceptional people.

The campaign headquarters were a loan from the family of Jim Holt's boyhood friend, Jim Bob Duggar of "Nineteen and Counting" fame. In exchange, the Holt campaign was to renovate it. A lot of time and energy was spent on that building. I kind of wondered if we would be better off without a fancy headquarters. The best asset we had was an extremely personable candidate, and I thought we needed to focus on getting him out among people.

Josh Duggar was also on that campaign and I got to know him. I saw no hint of his later troubles in those days. I did see a cocky teenager, but there was a lot of that going around. He more naturally gravitated to Jason than me because they as a family valued being able to do things with one's hands. I ribbed Jason about the way Josh followed him around even though he was sometimes grumpy about it, especially when Josh's overconfidence caused him to ignore Jason's warnings and start on a complicated IT project that Jason had to fix and then finish. It was all in good fun though.

The stereotypes of a narrow cultural mindset may have been more applicable to the Duggar side of things. Though I was attracted to many things about their choices, even then I questioned some of the Bill Gothard teachings. I thought it focused on works to the point where it was sold as almost being able to expect certain outcomes from God in exchange for one's performance. I felt this view infringed on the sovereignty of God and was akin to "magic". When Josh graduated from homeschool, I bought him a book by C.S. Lewis. This wasn't on their approved reading list and he made it a point to tell me that he didn't read it! It was a shame because performance-based religion doesn't renew us from the inside. Only His grace can do that as we come to fully understand how complete it is. If that's not the focus, it isn't what I believe. Even if you slap the label "Christian" on it, it becomes something else.

At any rate, the campaign ended and winter came. I sold furniture and lived my life. After the campaign ended, Jason Sheppard and I stayed in touch. In fact, he decided to join the Constitution Party in 2005, after the Holt Campaign ended. Melissa helped plan the Convention in Little Rock where I officially handed the Chairmanship to Jason. I was still an Officer, but he was in a much better position than I was to build the party. I was ready for some help, and to focus more on my new life as a husband and hopefully father.

Sometime in the midst of all of this, the few Constitution Party members who were willing to do some work tried to get the Constitution Party on the ballot. Except for President, which required only 1,000 signatures and the national party jumped in, we failed miserably. In the meantime, the national party was always suggesting that we do this or that, and except for getting their presidential candidate on the ballot really were no help. They expected us to pay fees to them and send people to their quarterly conventions. It began to dawn on me that having a national party was a drain on efforts to start a state one.

I had noticed from following the laws on ballot access that Arkansas was a "repeat offender". That is, the Federal Courts would rule one provision or another in Arkansas ballot access law unconstitutional, and they would order it stricken. Maybe ten years would go by and the legislature would re-enact the same provision which had already been declared unconstitutional. This would last until someone took them to court again, at which point it would be struck again, until the next time the courts were not looking.

One of those provisions was the terms under which new parties could get access to the ballot for their candidates. The law had said that 3% of the voters needed to sign a petition saying they wanted access. That was over twenty thousand voter signatures and there was only two or three months to collect them. A court ruling in 1996 had a footnote saying this was unconstitutional. The courts had consistently ruled that ballot access law couldn't be onerous just because the two dominant parties wanted to keep competition off the ballot. Ten thousand signatures was all it took for a single independent candidate to get state-wide ballot access and the courts suggested that this was a more reasonable limit.

I drafted a bill which would change the number of signatures all the way down to 7,500, hoping that 10,000 would be seen as a "compromise". In truth, moving the signatures required to 10,000 was just complying with prior court rulings from the federal court. Complying with courts was a big deal at that time because the State Supreme Court ruled that education funding was "unconstitutionally low" and ordered the legislature to spend more money on public schools. I thought that it was ridiculous bench-legislating and that one could not lay a finger on the provision in our state constitution mandating any specific level of funding. It was up to the legislature. But the legislature and the Governor fell all over themselves in the name of "complying with the courts".

They used the ruling to push through a bunch of measures that their constituents didn't want, including school consolidation, with the excuse that they were complying with the court ruling and had no choice. When Holt wondered aloud about "Separation of Powers" the state-wide newspaper ran one of their usual despicable unsigned editorials bashing legislators who even dared voice the opinion that they should listen to their constituents and that maybe it wasn't the court's business to decide how much money to spend on schools, but rather the job of the legislature.

I can't remember if any other legislator stood with him. Probably not. They wanted to be seen in the newspaper as champions of the people and of the constitution. And the way you got in the newspaper as said champions of the people was to sell out the people and ignore your oath in favor of what the people who ran the paper wanted!

At any rate, that was just a state court which had ruled for more school spending, and the Governor and the legislature were jumping through their own anal cavities to "comply". Arguably they were just using the court ruling as an excuse to ram through some unpopular measures that major players in the state wanted done anyway- like consolidate smaller school districts, but this was their stated reason.

Nevertheless, when Jim Holt presented his "Equal Ballot Access Act" to change state election law so that it complied with what *Federal* Courts had said, they wanted nothing to do with it. The bill died for a lack of a second. Not one Republican, or Democrat, spoke up for the bill. Holt told me that the Chairman of the Republican Party at the time, then-Senator Gilbert Baker, gave him grief for even running the bill. Complying with the courts only mattered when it was something they wanted to do anyway. When it came to competition for their jobs it was a non-factor.

I will just skip ahead and tell you that the next year the Libertarian Party of Arkansas sued the state over the ballot access requirement, and the Federal Courts again ruled that the 3% requirement was excessive and ordered the limit be reduced to 10,000 signatures. Exactly what Holt told them would happen based on what I showed him. I believe the state had to pay all court costs. I don't think they cared, it kept competition off the ballot for a while, and taxpayer money was no object for them when it came to protecting the privileged ballot position of their two parties.

Chapter Eight

The Campaign for Lt. Governor and Moving On

Around the Fall of 2005 I got a call from my friend Jim Holt. He was trying to figure out what to do next politically. He could run for his State Senate seat again, but he wasn't enjoying it because all he could do was play "spoiler". That is, he could call attention to crooked deals and bad bills and stop them, but he had great difficulty getting anything passed. The people floating the crooked deals and bad bills didn't appreciate his "grandstanding", or whistleblowing is the way you or I might see it.

Some people were urging him to run for Lt. Governor. Some were even urging him to run for Governor since Mike Huckabee was leaving due to term limits. But Asa Hutchinson was itching to run for Governor and Jim told me that a couple of key legislators close to Hutchinson, bonified insiders, were saying they would support him if he ran for Lt. Governor instead. That was potentially "big", maybe even a breakthrough if the party finally really got behind a true grassroots guy. He wanted my opinion on it.

The Lt. Governor Campaign and Moving On

I urged him to run for Lt. Governor too. It was a bigger platform and his ideas had always been more important than any particular bills that he might have. He eventually decided to do that, but he was really torn. He finally said that he would if I would serve as his Campaign Director. I said that I was working a lot of hours and there was no way I could do the job well enough. He said that he anticipated raising more money this time around, and thought that he could afford to pay me a survival wage if I would work for him full time.

I thought things over. I had some very generous friends in my life at that time who out of the blue decided to gift me $10,000. Between that and things going well at work I had saved enough for a wedding ring and a respectable Florida honeymoon. I wanted to be ready to "pop the question" to Melissa when the time was right. Actually, I was already secretly communicating to my cousin in Texas who crafted jewelry about an engagement ring. But this offer was no kind of steady job. More of a hope or a gamble really. If he won and I served well, I figured there would be a place for me on his staff. That would be a dream job for me, or at least I thought so at the time. Melissa could tell I wanted to do it, and so she gave me the green light even though it was a huge risk.

I was selling a lot of furniture, but I had learned some things about the way the company operated that had bothered me. I had a gift of being able to connect with all kinds of people, and a big part of that is that my sincerity comes through. Over time I realized that some people who did not have that gift, because they were not sincere, used people like me to sell ideas and things. I had to learn over time when I was being drawn into a situation like that and find a way to move on.

There were also rumors afloat that the company was about to cut sales commissions, bringing it in line with most of their competitors. And the fact was, I could see more of Melissa on the campaign than I could stuck in the store half a state away because we would be in central Arkansas a lot. Add all of that together, and I decided to roll the dice. I told my boss, who by then had become a friend of mine, that I was giving notice. My last week on the job I was number one in the chain in delivered business out of a hundred and thirty-eight salesmen, but he understood.

I want to end this chapter with the biggest and best change of them all. I had decided to ask Melissa to marry me exactly one year from the date that I had asked permission from her father to court her. I had set my cousin (who was a jeweler) to work crafting a custom engagement ring. With my new job I had the flexibility to be down in Little Rock for that date. The only trouble was, my cousin wasn't one to stick to a schedule.

My calls to him grew increasingly frantic about the ring. Finally, we decided that if he mailed it directly to her parents' house, it could be there in time. I would come a day early and intercept the package. Then I would ask her to take a walk with me to the top of Pinnacle Mountain and propose. I drove to her folk's house in Little Rock and waited like a hawk for the mail. It didn't come. Our hike was scheduled for late morning the next day.

The day came and we got ready and walked out the door. As we were getting into the car to leave, the postman pulled up. I stopped to speak to him and sure enough, the package was there! I put it in my pocket and drove to the state park! It was like in a movie. Most things haven't worked out that smoothly for me, in case you are wondering.

It was a beautiful day for a hike up the mountain. It was a pretty vigorous climb but the air was sweet and the sky blue. At last, we reached the bench at the top and took in the majestic view. Under God, I am a pretty defiant person. I bow my knee to God regularly, to man never, and once, to a woman. That was when I pulled out that ring I had so carefully prepared and asked her to marry me. She was so happy, I felt like it was the very best thing that I had ever done. Political good is shallow and transient. This meant something eternal. She said "yes", and we talked about plans and dreams, and some just plain logistics. Then we prayed for her good friend to find her husband, or actually that things would work out for the one she already had in mind. It would be thirteen years before God answered that prayer in the affirmative, so sometimes the answer is "not yet", but that's another story. We walked down that mountain as betrothed.

The whole family rejoiced at the news when we returned. That was pretty big of them considering I was a guy in my forties who didn't have a real job. They quickly shifted into making wedding plans and we set a date of March 11th. That was less than three months away. I didn't have an appreciation then for the immense logistical effort it took to go from zero to respectably fancy wedding in that time frame. Well, I don't guess she started from zero. Later she confessed to me that she had bought her wedding dress two months after we started courting! She was way ahead of me.

The campaign situation was very much unlike Jim Holt's U.S. Senate race in 2004. The wheeler-dealers who ran the state party on behalf of the big-money people hadn't cared a bit who ran against Blanche Lincoln, because they figured the challenger had no chance. But the 2006 race for Lt. Governor was different. There was no incumbent, the Democrats were reeling, and the Republican brand was coming on strong in Arkansas. For the first time in a long time, it mattered who the Republican nominees for state offices were. The establishment went from "malevolent neglect" to more active, if still clandestine, measures to stop guys like Holt from securing "their" party's nomination.

When the establishment was trying to discourage Holt from entering the race, the buzzword that they repeated was that Holt would "drag down the whole ticket". It was an excellent example of how stupid "experts" are. Holt had just finished getting more votes than any Arkansas Republican in the history of the state up to that time other than Win Rockefeller. It was G.W. Bush who would drag down the ticket, but these same fellows fawned over him. I mentioned to my friend John Barry Baker about these chattering insiders whining that Holt would "drag down the whole ticket". He said, "Holt will drag *up* the whole ticket, just not enough to matter."

The grassroots were filled with a lot of "Salt of the Earth" kind of people. These folks had lived good lives and were very capable. But for the most part their talents were not in running winning political campaigns of this scale. The kind of folks attracted to that line of work didn't last unless they followed the money, so the preponderance of that talent pool was going to back another candidate, not Holt. This is why he had to resort to someone like me and my network outside of the regular GOP.

Heck, I was still a State Officer of the Constitution Party. We were just not going to get ballot access for our party, so the best we could do for the public good was work to elect an outsider Republican. At least that was my thinking at the time. Now I don't even vote in primaries because I don't want to do anything to encourage good people to enter the web of either of those corrupt clubs that have bankrupted America both morally and financially.

Not that the third party I was in was the answer. When I finally did get to go to one of their national conventions, in 2004, it only helped me realize that I didn't want these folks running the country either. My ideas about decentralization of political power were starting to take shape.

It turned out that the Constitution Party was composed of state parties from the old "American Independent Party" that affiliated with them for national purposes. That was the party that George Wallace ran under back when he was a segregationist. So already I didn't like them. It turned out that they were dominated by Mormons who were keen on changing the preamble to the platform that took an orthodox Christian view of Christ and making it something more generic that was acceptable to Mormons. They also

The Lt. Governor Campaign and Moving On

wanted to soften the pro-life plank to make it more in line with what the Mormon Church believed.

The California party was by far the biggest party of any of the state parties, on paper. But it was all smoke and mirrors. A lot of voters in California thought that they were registering as "Independent" but were actually checking a box for the Independent Party of California. So much of the basis for their clout, and their huge delegate block, was based on this fiction.

They were threatening at the convention to leave the party if changes were not made to suit them. That threatened the Constitution Party's claim to be the "largest third party in America". Since that claim was not based on solid numbers, and they were the remnants of a party who ran a segregationist for President in 1968, and they were demanding the platform fit with Mormon doctrine including on the pro-life issue, I was inclined to either call the bluff or let them go.

When I went to my hotel to go to sleep the night before the vote, I thought enough other state delegations were feeling the same way. Enough to make it stick. When I woke up, it turned out that national leadership had approached others and invited them to some after-hours meetings where a deal was cut, and the changes were made. I wasn't ready to leave the party yet, but let's say it tempered my enthusiasm.

Let's get back to the Arkansas Lt. Governor's race in 2006. Two other candidates entered the fray. One was an Attorney named Chuck Banks from the eastern part of the state. The other candidate was a state legislator who was also from Northwest Arkansas named Doug Matayo. Remember when I gave all the money I raised as a Republican to two Republican candidates? I told you that one of them very graciously thanked me (Jim Bob Duggar) and the other cashed the check and never replied? That other one was Doug Matayo. So let's say we got off to a bad start. He had a conservative record, but he played ball with the establishment when it mattered.

He had no trouble getting bills passed, in part because he ran the bills that the big boys wanted run. He was photogenic and charming.

Doug Matayo was just the man to cut into the vote from what would otherwise be the Holt base. Of course, from his perspective Holt was cutting into his vote. But the bottom line was that if they could force a run-off with either of those guys, the establishment probably figured they would be in good shape.

There may not have been a lot of establishment people compared to the grassroots, but politics was like both religion and business for them. Their personal interests were in seeing the system perpetuated. They would show up for a run-off. There would be no guarantee that Holt's grassroots, family-oriented people would even remember a run-off election for just Lt. Governor. It was hard enough to turn them out for the primary election with all kinds of candidates on the ballot. If they could just force a run-off, they had a good chance to do what I think a lot of them longed to do- embarrass Jim Holt.

So, he had two strong opponents who were of the right sort to "bracket" his support. Later events would reveal that the powers that be clearly favored them. Holt's optimistic views about being able to pay me evaporated quickly. The other two were the favorites among the few people who wrote checks for multiple thousands of dollars. No matter how upset the grassroots got at Holt's lack of support last go round, until the party picked a nominee, he wasn't due any help. He felt awful enough about it. So much so that between that and the next issue he seemed like he didn't want to run for a while.

There was another good reason his fund-raising was behind schedule: His lack of travel. It turned out that his wife Bobye was pregnant again. They had their children at home, unless there were complications, and she didn't want him to leave the county with her in her last trimester. I know that the perception outside of fundamentalist circles is that since the men are supposed to be the "head" of the family and that they dominate their spouse and lord it over them. That does happen, but such men tend to be social outcasts that few others respect.

The truth is that the way it often works out in practice is that the man is "in charge" of making sure his wife is happy! That's what he is "in charge of". Sort of like how Christ is the "head" of the church, but in practice He loved the church and gave Himself up for her. So, our candidate would not be leaving the county right up until the eve of early voting in the primary election! Our strongest asset, a personable candidate, couldn't leave the area to campaign. Meanwhile dates for the events that the County Committees were holding to showcase the candidates were fast approaching.

I had a tough decision to make. Do I go beg for my job back at the furniture store or do I cash in my pitiful teacher retirement and live off of it in the hopes that he won? If he did, there would be no shortage of players telling him how their check got lost in the mail and they were with him all along. He could pay me back. Plus, the Lt. Governor got to hire a small staff and I could be on it. After mulling it over, I decided to rather recklessly roll the dice. I was moved by the sacrifices I saw others making with their time.

We soon came up with a work-around for the fact that our candidate wouldn't be leaving his home county during the meat of the campaign while his two strong opponents were out barnstorming the state- I would fill in for him. This idea reeked of desperation, but it was not as stupid as it sounded. People wanted to see the candidate, and I could not work a room like Holt, but I was a superior public speaker in those days, with an agile debating mind. I knew the issues at least as well as he did, and the details much better because I was a wonk- a geek trapped in what used to be a jock's body.

If we did it right, people would leave the events with the idea of, "wow, even Holt's Campaign Director made more sense than the other candidates, how awesome must Holt be?" Holt would not have to drive across the state to ride in a parade in Jonesboro. The other candidates could wear themselves out doing that while I rode in the back of the car in a suit and waived. Add to it that if Holt really messed up and said something dumb, he'd be pilloried for it. If I did, Holt could just come out and say I didn't speak for him on that and get a "mulligan". The other guys were under this same restriction. They had to be more careful and measured in their words.

My new bride and I went all over the state for Holt that late Winter and Spring. We met a lot of salt-of-the-earth people and a few of the usual scoundrels that gravitate toward politics. I think it frustrated the heck out of the other two candidates. Maybe they thought at first that they would be a tough act for me to follow, because early on I found that I was speaking last. When it came down to it though, I seemingly on-the-fly effectively rebutted every point they made.

After that I noticed that things changed and I would show up somewhere and I would be asked to speak first. It didn't matter. It wasn't that I had been responding on-the-fly. I already knew "where they were going" with their speeches. It didn't matter if I went first or last. Metaphorically speaking, I could just hold up my fist in the right spot and I knew when it was their turn, they would walk right into it.

For example, Doug Matayo was a legislator who had gotten a lot of bills passed. My guy Holt was a legislator who only got a couple of bills passed into law. His strong suit was stopping bad bills that the establishment supported. That didn't win him many friends in the ledge. He was almost like a whistle-blower on the bad bills and sometimes he would be the lone "no" vote. But I was able to sell the idea that we needed a contrarian to counter all the "go along to get along" in the legislature. I said "the number of bills passed with one's name on them isn't a good measure of a legislator, because our problem isn't that we have too few laws, but rather too many." The crowds loved it. It totally neutralized Matayo's appeal, turning it into a Holt-Banks race. Naturally his folks were fuming.

Finally, there was an event in the River Valley where for the dinner portion they had a long row of tables on the stage, elevated above the crowd. That was where the important people sat, including Banks and Matayo. I was relegated to one of the tables in the crowd. The message was pretty clear- here are the "approved" candidates and that guy who is "representing" that outsider candidate isn't worthy of the stage.

To further point out that Holt was not there and his designee was unworthy of being among the great men's table, when the host introduced me to give my talk (from the floor, not the stage like the rest of them) he offered an "apology" with a Cheshire-cat smile that there wasn't room for me up there. I stood up and told them all, "There is no need to apologize. This is exactly the way things should be. Jim Holt is a man of the people. As his representative this is where I belong, down here with the grassroots." They withered.

It was at that same event that Banks said from the podium, "You are right Doug, we need to talk about this Constitution Party stuff." Well, that was a shot across my bow, because I was still an officer of the Constitution Party going around to all these Republican events speaking for a candidate in their primary. Afterwards someone from the crowd asked me if I was in the Constitution Party. I sheepishly said that I was and they said, "No, it is nothing to be ashamed of. I like the Constitution Party." Some of the grassroots at least was tired of officials from their party talking one way but governing another. Still, I could tell that it was time for Holt to get back in the saddle and me to quit playing candidate.

The thing was, Holt loved things the way they were. From his view, he was winning the battle without ever having to leave HQ.

At first, he said he had to stay because the baby was coming, then it was because he had a newborn. It became a point of friction. I was out there and as good as I thought I was at it, it was time for people to see their candidate, not me.

He did get back in the saddle, but I still wasn't done being the candidate. Though the details were hazy, Bush Presidential advisor Karl Rove and Holt had some kind of tension going. I think it was on illegal immigration. At any rate, the party arranged for a huge fundraising dinner with Karl Rove flown in from Washington to be the Keynote Speaker. The candidates would get about two minutes each. It was a potential trap. It would be just the place for the establishment to spring an ambush and set up Holt as the guy who was ugly to the wonderful Karl Rove, who was their guest.

Our solution was that Holt would go to one of the other smaller events that were going on in the state that night, where he would have the whole floor and be the star attraction. We were not going to beg for a lousy two minutes at an event where the Keynote was a master strategist who could collude with the organizers to embarrass us. I went to the big dinner where Rove was speaking in place of Holt. They wanted to make a point that Holt was not there by calling out his name. I stood up and said "Holt went down to Crossett, they offered him *twenty* minutes down there!"

Truth was they offered him as much time as he wanted, but I had gotten a chuckle, made my point and gotten Holt off the hook for his no-show. It made the point that Holt was a valued commodity, and you could not expect a man of his caliber to show up for two minutes when there were plenty of people around the state that wanted to hear a lot more from him! It was like Ju-jitsu. The whole dynamic changed with those few words- Holt wasn't dissing them, they had dissed him by offering him only two minutes when he was the guy people around the state wanted to hear from- unlike these other guys that were willing to take any scraps thrown their way since listening to them was such a chore! All that, and we deftly avoided any traps that had been set.

He did get back in the saddle, but it really turned out that for us to stay friends, I needed to quit working for the guy. I thought of him as my client, and he thought of me as his employee. And either way I was not being paid but living off of our cashed-in retirement. I left the campaign right before early voting started for the primary but kept it on the QT for a while.

The primary election date rolled around and despite the establishment's best efforts, Jim Holt picked up 55% of the vote in a three-way race. There would be no run-off. If you have been following these things, you know that when an outsider candidate is losing to an establishment candidate in a primary, the compliant media demands that the outsider say whether they would endorse the establishment candidate in the general election. If the outsider candidate says "no" it is used as proof that they are not a "team player" who is committed to the party. If they say "yes" and then refuse to do it then they are pilloried for not keeping their word.

This is why you have good candidates asking their friends and family for money to pay party filing fees to run against some insider who is ignoring the party platform and just listening to the big money. Then they ask them for more money to buy tables at the fundraisers that the party keeps hosting.

If they do manage to beat the insider, they rarely get that money back. If they lose to the insider, the money they raised from their momma and their best friend goes to the insider who beat them, and they are put in a position where they have to endorse him to boot. I hate party politics! I think all legislators should be elected as independents who answer only to their constituents in their district, not some party headquartered in Washington D.C. and funded by global corporations. It isn't even American money that is buying these elections anymore!

At any rate, the media didn't badger the candidates in this race about it, because the outsider was winning. My experience was that the party had no problem with leaning on grassroots candidates who lost to insiders to endorse those insiders to "unify the party". The reverse is not true. Banks never did endorse Holt, saying that he had some questions he wanted Holt to answer before he would consider it.

That of course, was an insult on many levels, and Holt rightfully refused to beg Banks for something that, by the "rules of the game" he had already earned. So far as I know, Matayo never endorsed Holt by name. I could be wrong, but what I heard was that when pressed he said, "I endorse the Republican nominee." Of course, neither of them resigned from the party, which would have been the decent thing to do if you aren't willing to give a real endorsement to the guy who beat you in your own party primary.

So Jim Holt was the Republican nominee for Lt. Governor and Asa Hutchinson was the nominee for Governor. The thing was, Holt had the base way more fired up than Hutchinson did. Hutchinson has gotten better over the years, but he just isn't a warm or inspiring public speaker. Nor was there anything about his record that would lead people to believe that he would really stand up for them.

Remember the two legislators who were close to Hutchinson that Holt said would endorse him if he ran for Lt. Governor instead of running against Hutchinson for the Gubernatorial nomination? Well, neither of those guys backed Holt at all, and indeed appeared to do everything they could short of an endorsement to back the other Republican candidates for Lt. Governor. So Holt wasn't too happy with the Hutchinson camp at that point. Nevertheless, Holt held a big event and Hutchinson announced he was going to come, that it was in effect a joint event. If Hutchinson couldn't draw a crowd outside of the party insiders he could stick to Holt and Holt

The Lt. Governor Campaign and Moving On

could draw the crowd for him! Holt had mixed feelings about all this, but why not be nice and make peace if one can?

The state's biggest newspaper, the Democrat-Gazette, went ape over the news. They could not stand Jim Holt or more importantly what he stood for. Like most media, they were globalist. Why shouldn't they be? These days their biggest advertisers are global companies and most media is owned by global companies. You are never going to get fair coverage from them of candidates who want local control of schools, or any policy that decentralizes power.

Globalists are fundamentally opposed to letting people in each place decide what they want the rules to be for them. The global government folks want the rules to be the same everywhere so that they face no obstacles when they put the mom-and-pop's out of business. Enforced sameness is their idea of "freedom". They figure they are more "enlightened" than the rest of us so their values are right for all people and all places and times. In other words, the media tends to be elitist to the core, and as such they seem psychologically incapable of giving populist candidates fair coverage. They only like the masses when the masses are agitating for what the elites want anyway- sameness.

The idea that Hutchinson would buddy up to him was unacceptable to them. They ran an editorial basically warning him off associating with Holt. Then they ran a series of negative editorials against Holt. Because he was against welfare benefits for persons who were in the United States illegally, they painted him as a racist. Pretty soon, our "problem" took care of itself and Hutchinson separated from the Holt campaign.

You might think that even if the media was hostile to Holt, at least his own party would pull for him. You'd be way wrong. First of all, the outgoing incumbent Governor, Mike Huckabee, jumped into the fray. He irreverently said that "Holt didn't drink the same kind of Jesus juice that I do" because of Holt's stance against welfare benefits going to persons who were in the country illegally. I think he didn't like Holt because Jim really was the kind of person that Mike Huckabee pretended to be in order to get elected.

Once elected by campaigning with a populist agenda, he governed with an elitist agenda, including the school consolidation issue I've already discussed. Huckabee was sliding left to align with the amnesty-friendly views of then President George W. Bush. And Bush's performance in office was sinking the chances of the whole Republican ticket in Arkansas. People were mad at Bush. Eventually when Huckabee was running for the Republican nomination for President he feinted right again on borders. The man isn't short on brazenness.

As time went on and polls came out two things became clear. One was that despite the machinations against him, Jim Holt was the only state-wide Republican who was close enough to win. The second thing that was clear was that the Republican Party of Arkansas would rather be shut out and lose them all than have Jim Holt elected as the only state-wide Republican.

The Democrat candidate was a guy named Bill Halter. Halter wasn't the favorite of the state Democrats either. After living in D.C. for a while he basically flew into the state and announced that he was ready to be in charge. Much like Jim's situation, he was convinced to switch from campaigning for Governor to campaigning for Lt. Governor in order to let the party favorite Mike Beebe have a clear shot. The difference was that once he got the nomination, they really supported him.

As the election got closer, I helped the Holt campaign out when I could. My friend Jason Sheppard was running it, to the point of burning out. I went down to Little Rock and was Holt's "Body Man" for the debate, which I thought he won handily. Then I went to a Republican event in Washington County where I had to listen to the State Chairman and also State Senator Gilbert Baker brag about how much money he had raised for the party on his recent trip to Washington. You may remember Baker as the Senator that

The Lt. Governor Campaign and Moving On

cornered Holt when Holt sponsored a bill about ballot access for third parties. I pointed out that Holt was the only one in the polls who was close enough to win a statewide race for the Republican Party. I asked him point-blank if Holt could get some of that vast amount of money that he had just said that he had brought in.

Baker started backtracking and hem-hawing and said he had no control over where the money went. He was the State Chairman, if he didn't then who did? Was there anyone to appeal to or was it just a circle of fingers pointing around with no accountability? Later Holt made the same appeal to Baker privately, and was told that the money had to go to Asa Hutchinson because he was at the top of the ticket, rather than to Holt, who still had a real chance to win.

You may recall two years previously that Jim Holt was running for U.S. Senate and that *he* was the "top of the ticket" for Republicans in Arkansas. At that time, he was told they needed to put their money in races where they had the best chance to win, not the more prominent races at the top of the ticket. Now Holt was the one with the best chance to win, and the story became that the money needed to go to the top of the ticket. The common theme was that the party would not back grassroots guys like Holt, only the excuse varied. I was convinced they'd rather not have a Republican win a statewide office if it meant that Holt was that Republican.

Two years later a U.S. Senate seat was up for grabs and Gilbert Baker ran for the Republican nomination to get that seat. I can't help but wonder if he didn't want Holt as Lt. Governor because Jim would have been an obvious choice for that U.S Senate seat if he had been the only state-wide Republican. Maybe Baker wanted it for himself. He didn't get it. Neither of them did. In the years to follow, Gilbert Baker would fall terribly. Last I heard, he was under indictment for multiple felonies and had been caught driving while under the influence of meth.

Never mind asking the state party for money. Once we wanted them to send a FAX on our behalf to the state media. The day came and went and they never sent it. We called and got some lame excuse. The next day came and went and they didn't send it. We had to beg them for three days to send a FAX! It was a ridiculous low level of "support" for the only one of their state-wide candidates that had a chance to win. But it got worse.

They told Holt that their "opposition research" had produced some dirt on Bill Halter. Jim wanted me in on the call when they discussed it. It turned out there was some paperwork which could be interpreted to mean that Halter didn't pay some property taxes he owed in Virginia. It looked pretty shaky to me. I thought it was the kind of thing that could just be a misunderstanding and I said so. The young man from the party assured me that they had gone on the attack with less solid documentation than this.

Holt and I talked about it. He was a few points behind in the polls. This could have been just the *Deus ex Machina* he needed to come out on top. I was extremely skeptical, especially when I learned that the Republican Party didn't want to release this to the press, they wanted the Holt campaign to do it. Well, put this one in the burgeoning "sometimes I hate it when I'm right" files. Halter had a very reasonable explanation, and the state party slunk away and left the Holt campaign with egg on their face right before the election. They never took responsibility for the bad information. To this day I wonder if they didn't set him up, but arguing against that is the massive amount of evidence that they are indeed just that incompetent.

Meanwhile, even though Halter wasn't the Democrats' favorite guy, they could read the polls and they sincerely wanted a member of their party to win every contest. This was the only close race and it was the obvious place to channel extra money. They found a quarter of a million dollars and pumped it into Halter's campaign. The money was used to buy ridiculous negative attack ads terrorizing elderly voters into believing that if Holt got elected Lt. Governor of Arkansas, he would cut their Medicaid and Social Security. It was ludicrous to even think the Lt. Governor had any control over those federal programs. The ads could have been easily and devastatingly refuted- if we had any money to hit back with. We didn't and for sure no "journalist" from those very stations Halter was advertising on was going to come to Holt and interview him about whether the ads running on their stations were honest or not.

Holt lost the election. Even after the "help" from the Republican Party backfired on Holt and the Democrats' effective help for Halter, that race was still significantly closer than the others. But it didn't matter. In politics second place is the first loser! Did Holt have his faults? Sure, plenty of them, just like me and everybody else. But to this day I think a lot of the problem was that the crooks and enablers running things, who wanted to consider themselves as good men, couldn't stand Holt's radical honesty. They were happy to be rid of him. To confirm this, the pattern would repeat itself with other office-holders over the years.

Chapter Nine

Life and Politics

For a while I was just trying to focus on making a living. I tried selling health insurance and I flopped. Not for lack of effort. Sometimes you can chop hard, but no chips are flying. I remember one day as I was driving around trying to sell group health insurance to small businesses, I heard a commercial on the radio from the new Governor, Mike Beebe. It was all about how if you had a small business the government could get you subsidized health insurance for your employees! Talk about discouraging! But the fact is more and more of the economy is like that. People trying to make a living unconnected to the government have to compete with people and companies which are. Their taxes help subsidize their competition.

I wound up walking away from that and selling furniture again, with a different company. It was really a good job for the kind of job that it was. The hours were almost 9-5 and I was working with some folks I liked a lot. In fact, one of the old crew I worked with at the other store was the one who pushed for me to be hired. It wasn't all commission, so you could only make so much, but for the season of life I was in where I was just taking stock of things, it was a good job. It had just the right mix of physical activity and people-work. I continued to get better at interior design. When I first got in the furniture business I was like most other guys- I knew the names of maybe five colors. But when you have to put enough sets together and enough women come in the store with pillow cushions asking you to help them find the right rug, your brain reprograms.

I remember once we volunteered to loan furniture for a house showing associated with a Komen Foundation event. My manager Terry Douglass and I took a lot of time making that show house look great. My friends on the sales floor laughed at me for missing so much floor time to put that show house together. I had the last laugh though when someone bought the house and basically all the furniture that Terry and I had put in it.

It was while I was working there that I became a father for the first time. Since I was in my late forties, I was more than ready. Heck, I had felt the paternal urge even when I was teaching, but now I had a child who was strictly my responsibility. I wouldn't say it changed me, because my instincts were those of a protector, but it did help me to become better at being who I really am. Life within the walls of our little home was good.

Outside the home, the world was still going crazy. I finally cut ties with the Constitution Party. In fact, I waited until the right moment and got the state party to disaffiliate from the national party. It wasn't just me leaving, the state party left. I had hoped that over time they would split with the "American Independent" state parties that were founded in the Wallace-era and were run by some of the more extreme Mormons. Instead, their influence seemed to get stronger. The national chairman called Jason Sheppard and I to talk about it, but things were what they were. The problems seemed intractable.

At the time we cut ties not everybody in the party was happy about it. One fellow, Jimmy Johnson, decided to run for the state legislature as an Independent, since we could not do it in the Constitution Party. By chance, I happened to be at the state capital when he filed. The incumbent for that spot, a Republican State Representative named Mark Martin, went ballistic. The thought was that I put Jimmie up to it, but it was pure coincidence that we were in the capitol at the same time. Jimmy got about 40% of the vote. If Mark Martin had drawn a Democrat opponent, the conservative vote would have been split and he would have lost his seat. Martin was smart enough to know that.

After the election, Martin approached me. He wanted a "truce". Heck, I am always open to making truces. Christians are supposed to be blessed if we are peacemakers, right? It was actually the start of a long friendship but it was based on the wrong idea that I had been pulling some strings.

Over the years, we worked together on legislation. My sister has two children who have been diagnosed with autism, so I am particularly keen on helping people with handicapped children. There is no way her kids could have made it in a public-school environment. All kinds of things set them off. At the same time, there are various private practices that can help them learn life skills that will make house calls or put them in a quieter and more intimate environment where they have a chance to learn something. I drafted a bill that would take the money that the state gives to the school district and put it in an account so that the parents of children with handicaps of that nature could pay people to educate their child in a more suitable environment.

Mark Martin sponsored the bill. But typical to his fiscal conservative roots, he refused to do so unless it was scored as Revenue Neutral by the budget office. They did score it that way. After all, they used static accounting to evaluate all of the bills, that was their policy. Static accounting assumes that people don't change their behavior due to the government program. If an autistic child was getting services from a school and instead, they got services from an equal-sized budget that was done elsewhere, no more money should be spent. The projected cost of the legislation was zero dollars based on the static accounting they always used.

Some education bureaucrats terrified the legislators out of giving the bill a "do pass" by lying to the committee that the bill would endanger federal dollars from various special ed programs. Not just the dollars going to a specific child, but would put Arkansas in violation of federal guidelines for all of the aid. Based on that lie, the committee voted it down. Mark Martin asked that instead of the bill being killed, it be placed in a study, to examine these claims more closely. That's where bills go to die, but as a courtesy they granted his request.

We took the study seriously though, and found a lawyer, Greg Brown of Bentonville, who put a legal opinion together for us. His work made it very clear that the claims were untrue. In the meantime, we submitted a series of questions for the State Department of Education to answer regarding services for children with Autism. That was a part of the process, so we were doing it on behalf of the committee. These questions put them in a difficult position, or excuse me, they put themselves in a difficult position by misleading the committee and basically doing a terrible job of helping children with these sorts of disabilities.

The bureaucrat who was running this effort even visited my sister at her home and offered to give her children special help if she would just drop this. My sister would do almost anything for her children, but she wasn't going to do that. We persisted and finally the education committee met again, this time in Fayetteville. We both spoke before the committee, along with Greg Brown. My sister was way more impressive than I was but I did mention that the state department of education ignored the questions that they had asked them to answer. The committee voted that we were correct on the question and the State Department of Education was incorrect. That didn't get the bill passed, but a short time later we heard that the Department of Education employee responsible for this trouble had been terminated. I have no idea if our battles had anything to do with it.

Two years later, Martin submitted the bill again. There may have been one insignificant language change but otherwise the bill was identical to the one he sponsored two years previously. This time, no one from the Department of Education was anxious to take on the bill. But the system still had its ways. They wanted the money to always always always stay in their hands and under no circumstances share control with the parents.

This time, when the budget analysis came back, they claimed that passing the bill would cost the state a huge amount of money. Maybe $20 million dollars every two years. It could have been more. Mark Martin wasn't fooled in the least by this tactic, but many on the committee were put off by the cost. I took a closer look at the numbers. It turned out, for perhaps the first time in state history, the bureaucrats responsible for scoring the cost threw static scoring out the window and used dynamic scoring.

That is, they estimated the number of autistic children that were in the state that had been pulled out of public schools and assumed that many of them would sign up for this program. Thus, the program would cause the state to spend more money- because it would be serving more children. The state would be spending that money because instead of violating the state constitution's requirement to provide a suitable education for these children it would then be complying with the constitution. That's the only way it would cost more. But besides that, I caught them using double-counting on most of the cost.

I told all this to the committee in my testimony and suggested they should keep this budget scoring report as a souvenir because it was the only time in their careers they had ever seen, or may ever see, a report of this kind which used dynamic scoring rather than the static scoring used for all other cost estimates. The budget department knew they had a problem and the young lady they first sent to present this to the committee was replaced by a senior budget official by the end of the day. But it didn't matter how much gravitas he had. The facts were against him.

At this point, some Democrats were swayed. It appeared that the bill had the votes to get out of the committee with a "Do Pass" recommendation. That is when Representative Tracy Steele, I won't forget this, looked across the room at one of his colleagues and made a side-ways movement with his eyes. Then they both got up and left the room in the middle of the proceedings. Without them, the room lacked a quorum and so no "Do Pass" recommendation could be given regardless of the vote. Martin was done in the legislature after that term, and my sister's children were "aging out" of this category, but I understand that a session or two later a much watered-down version of the same kind of program was passed into law.

By the time 2008 rolled around I was once again involved in Republican politics in a professional capacity. This gig didn't pay much, the good guys never seem to have much money because they won't sell their votes to the people with money. Still, I was working for my friend Jason Sheppard on behalf of a candidate I truly believed in. That was a guy named Ron Paul. Jason was his Campaign Director for the state of Arkansas and I was his Campaign Spokesman for the state.

Ron Paul was the wisest man to run for President in my lifetime. There is a video of him talking about various economic crises decades before they happened. He would say, "Because we are doing "X" it is going to result in "Y"". Sure enough, "Y" would happen. He could see things coming that others couldn't see. But the problem with being able to see too far ahead is that those of lesser vision think you are hallucinating. By the time what you warned about comes to pass, shallow people forget that you called it because they have already written you off as "that nut who hallucinates." But too many people didn't want wisdom, some preferred bombast, others tall handsome guys with a resonant voice. They wanted to hear their existing prejudices confirmed, not learn what they needed to learn in order to set their posterity free.

Of course, the media was against him because they want globalism with uniform rules for all the earth, devised by elites who feel qualified to manage every area of your life for you. He believed in bilateral trade, not corporations getting together and over-ruling national governments through multi-lateral "trade agreements". Ron Paul believed in rolling government way back and returning a lot of decision-making power to individuals. He would say "I don't want to run your life, I don't know how to run your life, and the Constitution does not permit me to run your life." The would-be god-men who wanted to run your life, the DC-elites and their busybody minions, just couldn't stand hearing talk like that.

He was described as "Libertarian-leaning" and that was one of the few things they said about him that was true. I leaned that way too, at least for central government policy. I thought most of the rules should be made at the local level. That way if I don't like them, it would be easier to either get them changed or move a few miles where I liked the rules better. Later I would refine and define this idea better, calling it "localism" as a philosophy of government.

Ron Paul also talked about the Federal Reserve System, and how giving them the power to create unbacked fiat money would lead to disaster. With his track record, I thought people should listen and the more I investigated it the more I realized that honest and decentralized money was one of the most important things necessary to maintain a free society. Under our current system, the big banks have access to almost unlimited free money. If they stupidly make losing bets, they get refinanced with public credit and can go "double or nothing" until they win. If the rest of us behave stupidly, we lose our house to those same banks. Obviously, over time central banking will result in those connected to the central banks owning everything and the rest of us owning nothing regardless of merit. Good monetary policy is of paramount importance- second only to personal virtue in the citizenry.

Unfortunately, we don't have either of those things enough to matter in my opinion, and the Ron Paul race demonstrated that. Few people have the power to resist the allure of "free" money for very long. We didn't get in this mess overnight and we won't get out of it overnight- or without pain. Too much of our economy has been built around the distortions caused by government spending. The best we can hope for is that we wake up and voluntarily unwind from it in a way that minimizes the pain and sets the stage for a future lasting prosperity. Thomas Jefferson called it long ago when he wrote to John Taylor "The system of banking ...... I contemplate it as a blot left in all our constitutions, which, if not covered, will end in their destruction." Well, we ended it a couple of times but in 1913 it came back like a vampire and we've not found the integrity to put a stake in its heart since. Meanwhile, we get poorer and poorer and those connected to the banks and the government get richer and richer.

The problem with Paul's campaign wasn't his stance on central banking. It was probably the reason that the establishment loathed him and the global corporate media would not give him fair coverage so long as he was a threat, but it wasn't the reason he lost the race. In my view the root problem was that too much of the GOP base liked their candidates to be tough-talking ignoramuses. That or they needed to look great in a suit and have a smooth voice. They didn't want to have to change their mind about anything or the government to change its behavior. They just wanted FEDGOV to treat *them* differently. They figured FEDGOV didn't need to change a thing in the way it was treating the citizens of the nations that we were garrisoning.

Paul was arguing for a non-interventionist foreign policy. Not isolationist, but non-interventionist. He wasn't saying that we quit trading with the world, but that we quit trying to rule the world by sending our service members to every mud-hole on the planet. We shouldn't force other nations to embrace "our" vision of society at bayonet point. For some reason the same conservatives that resent FEDGOV here at home think that this very same FEDGOV makes great decisions running other people's lives in foreign cultures that they know even less about.

I remember this one Republican County meeting in particular, I was there speaking on behalf of Dr. Paul's candidacy. When I got to his foreign policy and said we should get out of Iraq the temperature in the room changed. One fellow kept badgering me, insisting that withdrawing our troops from the theater was going to get our troops killed! Somehow, getting them out of the middle of a 700-year-old Islamic Civil War between Shia and Sunni was more dangerous for them than leaving them there year after year. That was in 2008. It is twelve years later, and they are still there with more getting killed and maimed every year. Why?

It didn't get any better in 2012 even though the Republican base had four years of reality smacking them in the face to show how right Ron Paul was. I remember watching a Republican Presidential debate in South Carolina. When Ron Paul cited the Golden Rule and connected it to how we should treat other nations, those fine upstanding conservative Christians booed him! For citing the Golden Rule! Look, I know Islamofascists are dangerous, but what do you think God would rather us do, bomb Muslims or convert them? Well, we are already converting them, just not to Christianity. Lots of 'em probably had no thought of joining a Jihadi group until we blew up their house with their family in it. People who believe in limited government need to apply their principles to that government program called "war". There is a limit to the good that government action can do.

We did the best we could, and had some victories, but not enough. It was a crowded field at that point. Jason and I hoped to get Doctor Paul in the top three vote-getters in the state and hold favorite son Mike Huckabee under 50%. If no candidate got over fifty percent, the top three candidates were apportioned the delegates by a formula. He could still come out of the state with at least one delegate. Huckabee did finish under a little under 50%, but Ron Paul finished fourth, just out of the delegate allotment.

It is beyond the scope of this book to talk about the extreme measures that the Republican establishment took to freeze Paul out, both in this campaign and in 2012. But I will say that in a way his efforts contributed to the success of Donald Trump's campaign. Paul had some very diligent and dedicated partisans who studied the rules in their states and worked their way up the hierarchy until they were in position to help pick delegates. I think by now the GOP has bought off or run off most if not all of the people that Paul attracted to the party.

These arcane rules were probably meant to keep everyone but the insiders out of the picture. Once the system realized that this process could be used against them, they went the other way- for example instead of a caucus to pick the delegates, they would go more toward a primary. This paved the way for the opposite to happen later. Someone who could bring in a lot of new voters who didn't care to learn or finesse the rules but would show up to vote could change things fast. Donald Trump, a guy with tremendous name recognition and lots of supporters who were not system players and did not know the party rules, won the nomination. In their efforts to stop a candidate like Paul, they changed the rules in ways that favored a candidate like Trump. The response to the Paul campaign actually paved the way for Donald Trump to take the GOP nomination- and I don't think they liked it either way.

In 2010 I also had a small paying gig for a very nice man who was running for Congress as a Republican. He actually had some of his own money and I thought he was a good candidate, but he listened more to out-of-state political consultants than he did me. He lost but stayed active in politics, and wound up a Mayor of a nice small town. Those were side-gigs of course, and my day job was selling furniture, at least until 2011. When I go to 2012, I am skipping ahead in the story a bit. Let me back up because we skipped over The End of the World as We Know it and the rise of the Tea Party.

Chapter Ten

The End of the World as We Know it

The revisionist history is that the Tea Party got started because people objected to the election of Barack Obama and his health care plan. That's not the truth. I should know, I was right in the middle of it. I can see why those in charge of the present system and their acolytes in the corporate media would want to push that narrative, but it wasn't so. What got the Tea Party started was outrage over the massive bailouts that the big banks received starting in 2008.

The big banks made a vast amount of money by risky over-leveraging. That is, they would use every asset they had to give themselves as much credit as possible and use it all to buy more assets. Then do the same thing with those assets. When asset prices are going up, it works great. But it is also grossly irresponsible because when asset prices drop even a little then every investment in the chain of acquisitions becomes worth less than what you borrowed to buy it! When asset prices go down and you are leveraged 80-1 then your company can be worth billions one week and have a negative net worth of billions the next.

The politicians didn't do much to curb the over-leveraging because it would have slowed down the economy (to sustainable levels based on real production, not manic increases in asset prices based purely on easy-credit rather than fundamentals). So, they let the party go on until reality made it stop. If you or I overleveraged to buy assets that went down in value, we'd lose our homes. A lot of us did. But not the big boys. They got rescued by the same politicians whose influence they had been buying for a long time.

The connected banks, not your local bank but the big guys, could take their losing bets to the Federal Reserve's "Discount Window" and sell it or get a loan against it as if it wasn't a losing bet. In other words, at above-market rates. This amounts to a gambler getting a line of credit that allows him to go "double-or-nothing" until he wins! Even the U.S. arm of foreign banks wound up getting in on the act. Massive amounts of the risk from their poor decision-making got transferred to the Federal Reserve's books.

Things have only gotten worse since then, not better. Recently (in 2020) they put in the final missing piece of the scam that allows them to transfer toxic "assets" directly to the taxpayers' books! They buy everything in sight with risky levels of leverage, and if it works out, they keep the money. If it doesn't, they take it to the Federal Reserve and ultimately the U.S. taxpayer. We wind up with their junk. I am still furious about it. If half the citizens of this nation understood it like I do, we'd have a revolution by noon tomorrow. They don't, and the big media isn't about to tell them.

At any rate, in 2008 the Republican President, George W. Bush, supported the bailouts. The Democratic candidate, Senator Barack Obama, also supported the bailouts. Almost all figures on both sides of the aisle who were not named Ron Paul supported them. Ron Paul said something like we need to take our medicine and we will have a rough time for a year but then things will get better- for the rest of us, not the guys whose greed put our whole financial system at risk. But the Uniparty voted to keep the fraud going in spite of their constituents telling them 50-1 not to do it! Naturally this can-kicking didn't solve anything and we are now entering an economic crisis that will be blamed on a virus but was in fact inevitable from the moment they decided to protect the criminals on Wall Street instead of the taxpayers.

Although most didn't get the depth of how ruinous and unjust this policy was, people were very frustrated. Conservatives were frustrated. Liberals and leftists were frustrated. Moderates were frustrated. People without a defined political philosophy were frustrated. Many people who identified with one of the two major parties felt like they were being ignored by both of them- because they were. It was one of the more blatant examples of something that is true day in and day out. Policy is what the global elites who fund both private political clubs called "parties" want it to be, not what most voters want it to be. The Democrats who were "party first" types were more willing to give their new guy a chance, but everyone else was "woke" to the fact that these parties did not really represent them anymore, if they ever did. This was the true original angst that drove the formation of the Tea Party movement.

Think about it, if the Republican Party had satisfied these folks, why bother to go outside the Republican party and start an ill-defined "Tea Party" movement? They would have just stayed with the GOP. Or, for the independents who got involved, why not just join one of the two existing establishment parties? The Tea Party didn't start as an adjunct to the Republican Party. It was captured by clever stratagems and turned to that purpose, and I think ultimately its co-option is what killed it.

I was there at that first big rally that the Tea Parties had, on April 15th of 2009. In fact, I was the wind-up speaker at an event held on the town square in Fayetteville Arkansas. It was a great feeling getting up in front of 1,500 other concerned patriots and encouraging them and being encouraged. Not everyone liked my speech though.

I didn't carry on about Obama, but I did mention that a government that forces all states to endure abortion wasn't just to start with. My point was that we had a wide-ranging problem with the federal government pushing immoral policy, and this bailout was another very big example of a problem that had been festering for a long time- the government was acting in a morally illegitimate manner.

Most cheered, but after the speech one young man approached me and chastised me for bringing "moral issues" into the discussion. I asked him why shouldn't the government be able to print up a trillion dollars in debt, stick it on the tab of his generation, and give it to their bankster "friends"? "Because it is stealing!", he replied. I said, "if moral issues don't count, then what's wrong with that?" I think I blew his mind.

At any rate, local Tea Parties started forming up in various locations around the nation. One group tried to claim the mantle of "Arkansas Tea Party" but the rest were fiercely independent in those early days. They didn't like the idea of someone claiming to speak for the whole state. I agreed, but I thought that the local parties should form a loose association. At an early meeting of Tea Party groups, I tried to make a case for that, but they were against it. One guy, Trevor Drown who later wound up as a Republican legislator, repeatedly interrupted and badgered me. As I remember, I didn't even get to finish making my case. As it turns out, I was kind of glad they didn't get together at that point. I really didn't want there to be any sort of situation where they could lose their independence, but maybe others did.

I was one of four people who helped start the Benton County Tea Party. Jack and Jan Lea and Dorothy Hesse were the other three. We called a big meeting. I drafted up a proposed constitution and printed a bunch out and placed them on tables. But I deliberately made it so that those of us running the founding convention would not be on the board of whatever came out of the meeting.

Over one hundred people came. The room approved the constitution and elected a board. I wasn't on it, though I was a community representative for Pea Ridge on the larger committee.

My desire was for other people to step up and take responsibility. I wanted to be a part of a band of brothers, not the "leader". It didn't happen. In that room a few people agreed to serve in the officer slots, but no one wanted to run for Chairman. Finally, a tall distinguished-looking man with a resonant voice agreed to serve and so he was elected chairman by default. Things didn't go well, and I can share with you where we went wrong, and where a lot of the Tea Party went wrong, so that next time another populist movement can avoid those mistakes. My first mistake was leaving the door open for opportunists rather than making an effort to find true public-spirited patriots to fill every seat on the Executive Committee- including Chairman.

We soon decided that the Benton County Tea Party would have three major areas of operation, with a committee for each one. One would be "Issue Education", another would be "Events and Action Group" which was basically organizing demonstrations and going to government meetings to watch government bodies in action, and planning public meetings aside from Issues Education. The third committee would be "Candidate Evaluation". I was appointed head of that last committee.

The county just south of Benton County was Washington County, which is where I spoke at that first big Tea Party rally. They had a new Tea Party group too. They were also one of the biggest Republican voting counties in the state. Together, at that time, those two counties represented almost half of the Republican vote in the state in a typical primary election. Benton County alone was almost a third! We had leverage, and we decided to use it. We decided to host a candidate forum and we asked the Washington County Tea Party to co-sponsor it, which they agreed to do. But in order to maximize our leverage, we wanted the candidates to answer our questionnaire as a condition of participation in the event. The Central Committee of the Benton County Tea Party voted to authorize the production of a questionnaire and make it a condition for participation at the forum. So far, so good.

The Candidate Evaluation Committee, which I chaired, met and we compiled a questionnaire that we wanted candidates for federal office to answer. Most of the questions were not based on specific policy, but how a candidate viewed keeping his oath to uphold the constitution and the limits on federal power. That was what the whole first section was about. On many questions, credit was given for more than one answer. No matter what the Chairman claimed later, I told him over the phone we were going to put a cover letter with his name on it when we mailed out the packets and he was OK with that at the time. The return address was to a teacher who was a member of our committee who would "score" the questions according to how we had rated the answers.

The politicians who strutted around publicly as champions of your liberty privately freaked out at having to answer these questions. Turns out I still have most of them, so I'd like to share them with you. I do this both so you can get a feel for the kind of questions we were asking and so that you can get an idea of what all of the fuss was about. For some reason, I don't have all the questions, but this was the first half of the questionnaire anyway.

Directions: Circle the answer which best describes your views. Pick only one answer. The Candidate should initial the bottom of each page.

Section One: Candidate Views on the Constitution

1. Which best describes your view of the Constitution of the United States?

A. It is the highest law of the land and powers not expressly given to the Federal Government in that document are prohibited to that government.
B. The Constitution is still binding, and everything the Federal government does
must have some reasonable connection to a power positively granted to it by the
Constitution.
C. It is an honored document in our history, but its role has largely been eclipsed by Court rulings and our changing societal imperatives.
D. The Constitution is a document of negative affirmation, that is, if it does not prohibit the Federal Government from doing something, then that should be interpreted as giving the Federal government Constitutional authorization to do it.
E. Though a useful reference, it is not strictly binding on us today.

2. The legitimate meaning of the Constitution is best determined by using the standard of...

A. Whatever the Court says it means today.
B. What can best serve our society today.
C. The original intent of its authors.
D. The expediency of the situation.
E. Viewing it as a "Living Document."

3. Evaluating the Constitutionality of some government action...

A. ...should be left exclusively to the courts.
B. ...is the responsibility of every official who takes an Oath to defend the
Constitution.
C. ...is the exclusive responsibility of the Federal government.

D. ...is best left to experts.

4. The Ninth Amendment reads, "The enumeration in the Constitution, of certain rights, shall not be construed to deny or disparage others retained by the people." Pick the statement below which best reflects your view of the proper meaning of this amendment.

A. The Federal government is empowered to intervene against state governments to protect the rights of the people even if that power is not explicitly listed in the Constitution.
B. Federal power against the people is not just limited by the things listed in the
Constitution, but the people can possess other rights, not listed in the Constitution, which limit the power of the Federal government to intervene in their lives.
C. The Federal government is empowered to intervene against one group of citizens in favor of another group, even if that power is not explicitly listed in the Constitution.
D. This is where the right to health care and affordable housing can be found.

5. The Tenth Amendment reads, "The powers not delegated to the United States by the
Constitution, nor prohibited by it to the States, are reserved to the States respectively,
or to the people." Pick the statement below which best reflects the proper meaning of
this amendment.

A. The Federal government can only exercise its just powers on areas where the Constitution gives it specific authorization to do so.

Otherwise, the power to perform a given function is to be kept at the state, or even individual, level.
B. The Federal government is to serve as a sort of "referee" to decide when a power is to be exercised by the states or when it is to be exercised by an individual person.
C. This clause must be considered in light of the body of court rulings which have expanded the role of the federal government over time.
D. While "A" is true, the general welfare clause gives Congress broad authority to act in almost any area.

Section Two: Questions on Article One, Section Eight.....

Questions for Section Two:

6. The phrase "for the common defense and general welfare" means

A. Congress has broad authority to do whatever it thinks is good for the common defense and the general welfare of this nation.
B. Congress can do whatever it thinks is good for the common defense general welfare of the nation, unless it is an action specifically prohibited to it elsewhere in the document.
C. Congress cannot do anything it thinks is good for the "common defense and general
welfare," but is only authorized to do the 17 things which are listed below the clause
for "the common defense and general welfare."
D. The powers associated with the clause are connected to the list below them, and anything Congress does must be reasonably connected to some item on that list.
E. That the courts have broad powers to determine the constitutionality of any action of

Congress.

7. When Congress is given the power to "regulate interstate commerce" this means.......

A. ...if there is any conceivable connection between an activity and interstate
commerce then Congress may regulate that activity.
B. ...if interstate commerce was involved in any prior step used to create some good or service, then Congress can regulate commerce in that good, service, or activity whether such commerce in that good occurs within or without the state in which it was created.
C. ...if there is a reasonable connection between an activity and interstate commerce then Congress may regulate that activity.
D. ...Congress may regulate an activity if the activity is interstate commerce.

8. If a firearm is manufactured and kept within the borders of a single state, Congress can legitimately use the authority of the interstate commerce clause of the Constitution to....

A. Mandate the registration of that firearm or its owner in a federal register.
B. Mandate both the registration of that firearm and assess a fee for a person to possess that firearm.
C. In addition to (A) and (B), the Federal government can prohibit the manufacture or possession of that firearm.
D. Do none of the above, as there is no interstate commerce involved in the activity.

9. When the Constitution grants the federal government the power to "regulate Commerce with foreign Nations, and among the several States" it demonstrates that....

A. Congress is here given no more authority to regulate intrastate commerce than it has to regulate the internal trade of another nation.

Section Three: Judicial Usurpation

10. A member of the Federal court, including the Supreme Court, is appointed to office...

A. ...until another administration comes to replace them.
B. ...for life.
C. ...during a period of good behavior.

11. Which of these acts by a member of the Supreme Court would you most consider bad behavior worthy of impeachment?

A. Soliciting a prostitute
B. Driving under the influence of alcohol.
C. Usurping the powers of Congress or undermining the freedoms of the people by issuing extra-constitutional rulings.
D. A justice fails to pay federal income taxes.

12. The phrase "High Crimes and Misdemeanors" is best restated by saying..

A. ...felony or misdemeanor crime
B. ...the phrase is deliberately left vague so as to give Congress broad latitude in determining what acts qualify for impeachment.

C. ...whatever it may mean, it shows that the standard is that the member must at least commit a common crime that qualifies as a misdemeanor.
D. A "high crime" is not an ordinary criminal offense, but an abuse of official power even if not a crime, while by "misdemeanors" it is simply meant that public officials can be impeached even for consistently having a poor demeanor, again even if they have done nothing against the law for ordinary citizens.

13. What are some things that you as a member of Congress would be willing to do when the courts usurp authority which the Constitution either delegates to the Federal legislature or reserves to the states or to the people?

A. Impeach and/or convict the usurping judge(s).
B. Use the Constitutional power granted to Congress to determine the scope of a court's authority to remove from the court's purview any consideration of an issue where the courts have usurped.
C. Vote for a resolution condemning the courts for usurping the authority of the legislative branch, or of authority rightly left to the several states.
D. I am willing to do all of the above when a court usurps the authority of another branch of the federal government, or the authority of the several states.
E. I am not willing to do any of the above because I believe our rights are best protected by maintaining the independence of the judicial branch.

14. Which answer best describes your feeling towards the case, Roe v. Wade?

A. It is settled law, and should be upheld under the doctrine of Stare decisis

B. It is an example judicial over-reach and court usurpation of authority which constitutionally belongs to the several states, and should be overturned.

C. Constitutional or not, as a pro-life person I personally wish it were overturned.

D. As a member of the legislative branch, it is not my place to evaluate court decisions.

15. If you were a Senator voting to confirm a federal judge or Supreme Court justice, which would best describe your approach to using Roe in deciding whether or not to confirm a nominee?

A. I would use it as a litmus test in that any judicial nominee who did not think that Roe should be overturned does not understand the Constitution well enough to sit on a federal bench.

B. I would use it as a litmus test in that any judicial nominee who thinks that Roe should be overturned does not understand the Constitution well enough to sit on a federal bench.

C. Roe should not be used as a litmus test in either direction. A nominee's views on the case should not be a deciding factor in their confirmation.

D. Not that I am for abortion, but because Roe is settled law, I would consider their support of it in the interests of maintaining Stare decisis a plus for their nomination.

16. Which best describes your view toward the role of the doctrine of stare decisis?

A. Stability in law is so important that the doctrine should be adhered to even in cases where a questionable decision may contradict the Constitution, so long as the majority of the population is not concerned about it.
B. Stability in law is important, so I favor continuing the current policy of selectively using the doctrine of stare decisis in cases where the courts feel it should be applicable.
C. The doctrine should not be used as an excuse to uphold bad rulings.
D. The rights of the people are best preserved by being sure of what the law is. The people must know where they stand under the law, so maintaining this fundamental doctrine is probably the most important responsibility of the judiciary.

17. Imagine a scenario where a local official displays the Ten Commandments in the forum of the building where they work, and another scenario in which a school teacher uses a verse from the Bible to make a point in class. In both of these scenarios a federal court rules that these official's actions are unconstitutional violations of the first amendment. Your view on the matter is closest to which of the following....

A. Since neither of them are Congress, and their actions are not mandated by law, the courts have erred. Neither act violates the constitution.
B. As much respect as I have for the scriptures, the rulings are correct because it is wrong for agents of the state to use scripture in the course of their duties. This is a violation of the rights of citizens who may practice other faiths or have no faith at all. These rights are for everybody.
C. The courts should have let the local official display the Ten Commandments, because aside from religion the commandments are an important part of our heritage, but were correct in ruling

that the teacher's actions in front of minors was an unconstitutional establishment of religion.

D. I personally disagree with the court's decision, but this has been a long standing court doctrine and in the interests of stability in a diverse country I will respect the court's decisions.

18. In the Kelo decision the courts essentially ruled that one group of private citizens, or a corporation, can use the government to force other citizens to transfer their private property to the first group via eminent domain. Which statement best describes your views of Kelo and the use of eminent domain?

A. The courts have ruled correctly, one or two people should not be able to stand in the way of a development that can provide increased revenues to the entire city.

B. I disagree with Kelo and would like to see it reversed, if it is even a federal issue. Eminent domain should never be used to transfer private property from one private group to another.

C. The courts ruled correctly for state or local governments, but the Federal government should not be permitted to use eminent domain in this manner.

D. I am uncomfortable with this ruling. Going forward, I think we should pass legislation that prevents any further erosion of property rights.

Section Four: Executive Branch Violations of the Constitution

19. An agency of the executive branch searching the phone records of American citizens without a warrant is permissible....

A. If the Administration puts the citizens on a list of "suspected domestic terrorists".

B. If there is Congressional oversight of the program

C. Never, as it is a violation of the 4th amendment.
D. When the scope of data needed to secure our freedoms is so vast that it is impractical to get a warrant.

20. The government should be able to shut down or control access to the internet....

A. When Congress declares an emergency
B. When the President declares an emergency
C. Only after the Courts approve such a measure.
D. Never for qualified members of the media, because the First Amendment recognizes "freedom of the press."
E. Never period, because the First Amendment's guarantee of "freedom of the press" refers to a right possessed by all citizens, not merely those which the government designates as "journalists."

21. Pick the view that best describes your view of what limits could legitimately be placed on political protests by agents of the Federal government or state and local authorities operating at the behest of Federal officials.....

A. Law enforcement should have the power to order protestors into designated protest areas away from the path to an event so that political leaders do not have to face angry protests.
B. Law enforcement should have the power to arrest protestors for "disorderly conduct" should they fail to disperse from a peaceful demonstration on demand.
C. Law enforcement should have the power to bar entrance to a public event someone that they have reason to believe will cause a disruptive protest once inside the event.
D. Law enforcement should be able, depending on the circumstances, to do any of the things listed above.

E. Law enforcement would be violating the first amendment by doing any of the above.

22. What is your stance on reviving the Fairness Doctrine?

A. I agree it should be revived to equalize ideas deemed controversial on radio and TV.
B. I believe it constitutes a violation of the First Amendment and would have an adverse effect on free market principles and therefore should never be revived.
C. I believe it has merit but needs to be revised for today's media climate.

All kinds of people objected to our asking such "hard" questions. I remember this journalist, Jason Tolbert, asking me on my blog why I didn't let the candidates use their own words instead of forcing them into "best answer" multiple choice questions. He said candidates would prefer to "use their own words". Here was a "real" media guy, and there are a lot worse than him out there, believe me, who was chastising me for asking politicians questions that were designed to pin them down on difficult issues...in other words, for doing what guys like him should have been doing, but won't because they would lose "access" if they tried.

Here is how I answered him: Of course candidates would rather use their own words, that way they can leave themselves plenty of wiggle room. That way they can talk a lot and not actually say much. They can all imitate Mike Beebe and talk until they appear to be for all sides on every issue.

Yeah, they would rather use their own words, but not as a tool to help the voter know where they stand, but rather to avoid taking a stand. Almost all of those questions say something like "which answer *best* describes your views". Maybe none of them *exactly* line up with it, but the questions don't try to force that on them. Even if none of the answers *exactly* describes their view, one of them is going to be *closest* to their view. But it appears that they don't even want to be that clear with the voters on these fundamental issues.

Look, this little survey, which would probably take one of Jim Holt's teenage daughters 15 minutes to complete and get an "A" on, is just a jumping off point. If they want to add anything about any of these issues then great. Implying the survey is flawed because candidates can't use their own words is a false choice. They CAN use their own words to talk about these issues in venues beyond the survey. The survey is just a starting point to find out what side of some major lines they stand on. From there they can talk all they want about the details.

You think voters want to hear the candidates own words, so do I, but candidates are not saying anything of substance on most of these issues. They don't talk about it and they don't seem to want to talk about it. Every one of them from Nancy Pelosi to the Republican Senate candidates seem indignant at the very idea of telling us what they think it means to keep their oath to defend the Constitution. We don't know how they view the general welfare clause or the commerce clause. It is important to know.

We can't know what the issues of the day will be two years from now, but if we understand how the candidate thinks, what their principles are on the role and limits of the federal government, then we can judge how they will react to yet unknown problems.

****

Behind the scenes a lot more was going on. The politicians were leaning on both our Chairman and the Washington County folks to not make answering that survey a condition of participation in the forum. We held another Central Committee meeting and the Chairman demanded that we retract making sending in the survey a condition of participation in the forum. The Committee, fully aware of the contents of the survey, voted again to make answering our survey a condition of participation in the forum. Regardless of the vote, he told the group that he would "dig his heels in" against the candidates being forced to answer those questions in public. The meeting ended in acrimony. The Chairman did not stop there though, he continued to lobby the committee members one by one in private. But he did something else too.

One candidate for Senate, a nice guy who was a political novice named Fred Ramey, sent in his survey to our scorer. Well, another candidate did too, but the Chairman drove to her house and intercepted it before she could score it. And the other candidates all sent their survey to him. And he told them that he would never release their answers to anyone! So, they "sent in their questionnaires" and met the conditions of participation but none of us would get to see them because they cut a private deal with the Chairman!

The candidates' priority was his priority, and that was to not give the media or the Democrats any information that could be used against them in the general election. But this could be used as an excuse to avoid taking any difficult stand, and I believe it is a prime reason while most candidates blather on and on but don't really say anything about any controversial issues. So, voters have to guess on hints who the candidate really is- and of course if the candidate fails to deliver on the anticipated performance, well, they never really said anything definitive anyway. That is the way the establishment candidates wanted it, it was the way the establishment media wanted it, and it was the way that our Chairman wanted it. It became about not causing any risk to candidates of a particular political party.

At the same time the Chairman told us he was "not interested" in participating in any protests or demonstrations, which is how the Tea Party got started. It was when typical, often middle-class Americans started protesting- and it unnerved the system. One of our three committees had a primary job of organizing demonstrations and it just had its legs cut out from under it! We were quickly becoming an ancillary of the Republican Party. In fact, a few members of the Republican County Committee started showing up at the meetings. Just enough to make being too hard on any Republicans controversial within the group. We were quickly going from watch dogs to lap dogs.

I demanded another meeting where a vote could be held about releasing those survey answers, but he made it clear that he would not do so no matter what. In the meantime, they had also "gotten to" our colleagues in the Washington County Tea Party. I later became good friends with some of these folks, but that night I don't have the words to describe my fury at them. Four days before our joint "Candidate Forum" they made four demands. If we did not accede to each of them, then they would withdraw their participation. One of them was that the Candidate Questionnaires would never be revealed! They were helping with the coverup. The other three demands were almost as odious and our central committee rejected them. Our big event was cancelled.

The lady who was supposed to score the questionnaires resigned from the Tea Party in disgust, as I did myself shortly thereafter. The work of the Benton County Tea Party was supposed to occur through three sub-committees. One was an "Education" sub-committee that never got off the ground. The other was the "Events" committee that quit protesting or demonstrating, and cancelled the "Big Event" and spiraled into inactivity. The third sub-committee was the one I chaired, Candidate Evaluations. It was the only one which functioned effectively, and therefore the system acted to destroy it. Without those things, the "Tea Party" was just a place where political groupies could rub shoulders with politicians and pretend that makes them important, instead of just a bag of tools.

The Benton County Tea Party very quickly became irrelevant because they were not doing anything that wasn't better done as a member of the Republican County Committee. It soon went defunct. A gentleman I know tried to reconstitute it but so far as I know it is nothing more than a Facebook Group now. The same thing with the Washington County Tea Party, though it had a longer heyday. Even then, that was because a man named Jeff Oland somehow wound up as Chairman. He thought outside the box and the group was able to become a focal point for true activists, not just cheerleaders and groupies from one party. Eventually though, he was ostracized by other Tea Party leaders and it too faded away. The other way some Tea Parties kept going for a while was to accept money and speakers from outside the state. In other words, they let pros working for the system set the agenda.

Soon it just became rallies talking about how bad the Democrats were and telling folks that the answer was to keep voting Republican. In other words, they got co-opted. They could no longer act as an effective outside force on either of the two major parties, and they wouldn't sponsor independents to run for office where the major party candidates needed replacing. That's how the system beat the Tea Party, by simultaneously flattering and funding those who wanted to hobnob with politicians and scheming against and isolating those who wanted to truly hold them accountable on policy.

I don't just accuse the Republican side of the system- this one party with two faces that is really running America – of these things. House Speaker Nancy Pelosi accused the Tea Party of being "astroturf" or fake grassroots. At the time she first said it this was a lie. But the system was working to make it true after the fact. They could not have respectable law-abiding middle-class people protesting, especially protesting against the big banks and our fraudulent money system. In fact, soon after a movement called "Occupy Wall Street" came out of nowhere and they started making a nuisance of themselves. They were the real "astroturf" and I can't help but wonder if they weren't an evil but brilliant ploy by the system to turn Tea Party-type Americans against public protests.

The Soros-backed protesters interfered with public commerce, not just political events. They made left-wing demands that were loathed by the Tea Party folk. And right-wing radio show hosts that the system gave huge platforms condemned them as with one voice. Within six months, the same people who had gone to a protest themselves were calling for the police to crack down on the other side's protestors! As soon as the Tea Party went away as a protest movement, Occupy Wall Street also disappeared. I think this is because they had accomplished the purpose that their masters had for them at the time!

Some of you are thinking, "Mark that sounds like a conspiracy theory." Yep. Humans conspire. That's why there are laws on the books in every state against conspiracy to commit one crime or another. I'm not a "Coincidence Theorist" who thinks a large number of unlikely things just happened by chance to produce some convenient outcome for those with power. I think very smart people who have money and power are willing to conspire in order to keep it and get more of it, because that is the way human nature has been for all of recorded history.

One would have to be a gullible dullard to think otherwise, but many do because they have been trained by repetition and intimidation, not reason, to dismiss whatever the system calls "conspiracy theories." They are so timid they back down based on name-calling. Once someone calls a theory that, we are supposed to ignore any further evidence or reason which supports the theory and wave it away. "In politics there are no accidents," Franklin Delano Roosevelt once said. "If it happens, you can bet it was planned that way."

Was FDR a "conspiracy theorist"? Well, he got elected President four times, so if he was maybe we should be too.

Each "conspiracy theory" should be judged on how well the evidence supports it, neither accepted without good cause nor dismissed despite the data. Not that a conspiracy is always necessary. The late great George Carlin said "Where interests coincide, no formal conspiracy is necessary."

Since the Persians battled the Greek city-states it has been noticed that men who believe they are free work harder and fight harder and cooperate more with the system they are in than those who know that they are mere tools of the ruling class. Thus, clever overlords, and one does not stay an overlord long without some degree of cleverness, will find it in their interests for the common people to believe they have more say-so in the system than those running things are really willing to let them have.

Musician Frank Zappa put it like this, "The illusion of freedom will continue as long as it's profitable to continue the illusion. At the point where the illusion becomes too expensive to maintain, they will just take down the scenery, they will pull back the curtains, they will move the tables and chairs out of the way and you will see the brick wall at the back of the theater."

Chapter Eleven

The Illusion of Freedom

By 2011 my view of political representation had changed. I realized that national political parties were like any other institution. They can take on a life of their own with interests and goals which are different from whatever purpose they were created to serve, or whatever reasons the folks in the grassroots think it is about. The professionals who run the thing, and the bureaucrats that staff it, have interests which are very different from a grassroots person who wants certain policy goals. And if those goals are limiting government, forget it. The bigger government gets, the more important a successful political party gets. There are just that many more favors to sell. No matter what they tell you, the professional staff of a national political party that actually has control of government does not want government limited.

If a new party had any success, the top of the hierarchy could be bought off by the same money buying the other two off. Thomas Jefferson said, "God forbid we should go twenty years without a revolution." In terms of a peaceful revolution, in the sense of changing political labels when one goes bad, I was beginning to see what he meant. But we didn't just need one new political party, I figured we needed ten. That way, when one went bad, people could move to another one. This is the exact opposite of what we have now: Two clubs run by the same global money writing the rules to keep other groups off of the ballot, and to keep people from voting for them if they ever got on the ballot.

People have been trained to have a lifelong loyalty to one of the two parties and hate the other one. So, they tend to rationalize all the bad stuff "their" side does and vilify the other one for doing the same thing. It is totally unhealthy for the country, for the people, for everyone except those at the very top dividing us into two warring factions while they keep the looting going. Truth is, grassroots members of team red and team blue should both be after those running each of "their" clubs instead of at each other's throats. That's who is really putting the screws to both of them. But those on top didn't get there by being stupid. They know how to divide and conquer. They are masters of misdirection.

There should be so many viable parties that changing parties should not be a big emotional deal for people. It should be a normal thing for people to change parties four or five times in their life as they change or as the parties themselves do. It should be like changing brands of laundry detergent. If you use Red Bottle Detergent, you don't *hate* Blue Bottle Detergent or the people who use it. You just prefer Red Bottle. It can be that way when there are twenty other brands to choose from. All of Red Bottle's ad money isn't spent demonizing Blue Bottle or vice-versa. They don't tell you that the competitor's product is destroying the planet and therefore the people who use the other product are bad people. You are not terrorized into hating those who choose the other brand.

Instead of demonizing each other, they have to sell themselves because if they just went negative on each other all day people would get disgusted with the both of them and start using any one of a dozen other brands they could pick from. They could dare to look at their own side objectively instead of defend it to the hilt because the other side is the Devil's tool. What happens if they get disgusted at their brand now? They are trapped because they have been conned into thinking the only other choice is the scourge of humanity. The two-party system is completely toxic and needs to be destroyed for the sake of America.

Professionally, things were changing as well. Rick Candler, a friend I met in politics, had been trying to get me in the right-of-way business. This consisted of settling with landowners for oil and gas pipeline rights and things of that nature. I resisted because of all of the travelling, but as you know the folks running things got too greedy and crashed the economy in 2008-09. The furniture company I was working for finally went under in 2010. I quickly found another job selling office systems, cubicles, and things like that, but it wasn't a good situation.

I remember one day the newly elected Mayor of Rogers walked into the store. I had campaigned for one of his opponents. It was a contentious campaign. I realized if he knew I worked there he could probably use his influence to get me canned. That is a part of the reason for the herd mentality in the state. Petty payback is a thing. I am ashamed to confess to you that I basically hid from the guy. But I needed the job to feed my growing family. Or so I thought. When a proposed change to our system of compensation came down the pike shortly after that, it was the last straw. I was ready to go.

Providentially, when I came home that day frustrated and weary, Candler called me again and again suggested that I get into the right-of-way business. This time I said, "I'm in, who do I call?" He gave me a name and phone number. Four days later I was in rural Pennsylvania buying right-of-way. Even he was shocked at how fast it happened. These were not permanent jobs. It was a lot to ask of my wife. We basically lived in a new place every year and only went home between projects. A lot of women could not handle it, but she was very supportive. It helped that the pay was so much better that even a bad year in the right-of-way business was better than a good year doing what I had been doing.

Here I was in my late forties, and for the first time in my life I cared about money. I was a husband and father now and so I had to think more about the future, and more about providing for others. And for the first time in my life, I was making a good living. In addition to the pay, we got per diem.

It turned out that I was a natural at negotiations. It didn't matter if I was talking to a tenant farmer in his barn, or a fancy lawyer in the big city. This was a gift from my father, who was also able to connect to all kinds of people. I guess I got a little of it. I have been doing it for ten years and it has opened new doors for us, as well as allowed us to see a lot of the country. By the time my oldest son was five years old, he had been to the east coast, and the beaches of California, and the Gulf of Mexico, and peered out over the waters of Lake Erie into Canada. And we caught the best museums and science centers at every stop. "Moore Homeschool Academy" has a very enriched life-curriculum.

Another consequence of our fate playing out like this was that I was not reliant on anyone in Arkansas for my sustenance. They couldn't target my business or blackball me. My money came from outside the state. Heck, I rarely worked for the same outfit twice in a row, that's the way the business was. So, even if they had some connection with my employer, it would not matter. I'd just go to work for his competition. I was free to say or write anything I wanted to about Arkansas politics, and believe me I said and wrote plenty.

Early on, I had a project in Texas that was kind of messed up. They were paying us, but they didn't really have anything for us to do. That's when I wrote the first draft of "Localism, a Philosophy of Government." Heaven smiled on me again because it was almost like I was being paid to write! For the first time, I had the space to put all the big-picture ideas about government I had been thinking about into one document. Later I wrote a companion book to it, "Localism Defended" which ironically was more about the philosophy of government than the first one. I have hardly lifted a finger to sell those books, but that first one has been a steady seller for me all these years, because what it says applies just as much today as it did the day that I wrote it.

Writing the book helped me clarify my thoughts. I am not saying all of our problems in government are system problems. Obviously in a republic the virtue of the citizens is of paramount importance. There is no system one can devise that is so wonderful that it will give bad people good government. The best we can hope for is a system that can be reset easily when abuses grow too much, and that is localism as I have conceived it. Though the problems are not apparent to a lot of people, we now suffer from a terrible excess of centralization.

The system has been "fixed", in the negative sense of the word. Some of our problems are system problems, but I have concluded that many of them are a feature, not a bug for the people running things. Others are unavoidable consequences of having these deliberate flaws in the way we do things. That is, the folks running the show might not like it that their looting causes these problems, but they can't loot without causing them, and they sure don't want to be forced to make an honest living!

The best example I can think of is central banking. The central pillar of localism is that you cannot have central banking and a decentralized government. Indeed, you can't have central banking and a decentralized society in the long run. Those who control the printing press have a "magic money machine" which allows them to create buying power at will, by sucking it from the labor-value embedded in the currency held by all others, and give it to people and causes they favor. If you or I had control of such a machine, in time we would become all-powerful politically, and so must they. Therefore, if a nation is to remain free it must destroy the magic money machine of its ruling class and return to honest money.

People of great wealth can always buy themselves a loud voice, that's not what I am warning about. That's just the market in operation. What I am warning about is that once you have central banking the press-masters can shift the cost of shaping society to their whims onto the backs of the rest of that society. They can herd us as they like, and we will pay the costs of our own control.

For example, they could promote a particular social media company so that they achieve market dominance. And they could do this using money that they create out of thin air. Money whose value is ultimately drawn from the labor of the rest of us. If their venture is profitable, they pay the money back. If it isn't, they simply create more money and cover the losses. And if people resist the increasingly heavy hand of the manipulators and flee to other platforms, well once those platforms gain enough audience, they can simply buy those too. Then those with alternative viewpoints will have to flee again, and again, until there is no place to hide from those who have bought up the world with money whose value is obtained by the sweat of the very people that they are enslaving. There can be no living by "free market principles" when the associates of the press-masters have bought out everything and control all "private" property.

Aside from a lack of morality and public virtue, there is no bigger threat to our freedom today than central banking. It is the ultimate source of energy behind all other internal threats. Including the threat posed by social media herding. If neither dominant political party will address this issue, and they won't for their infrastructure has been thoroughly purchased by these same forces, then we need to migrate away from them too, just as we migrate away from social media giants. Even if we have to start one or one hundred local alternatives.

Here's another example: The Founders built this wonderful system of checks and balances, because they knew how politicians are. But the two-party system immediately sprang up, and it is nothing less than an informal end-run around the formal system of checks and balances that the Founders set up. They wanted state government officials separate from federal ones for example. But now politicians from both types of government are wearing the brand of the same party! They are working their way up the same hierarchy of this private club regardless of whether their goal is to be a Governor or a Federal Senator or whatever. A national party funded by global corporations naturally supports centralizing power, no matter what the Founders set up.

The same thing applies to the Executive Branch and the Legislative Branch. They were meant to check and balance one another. But when the Chief Executive is of the same party that controls the legislative branch, they don't. The legislature becomes mostly a rubber stamp. That is because the head of the executive branch is also the de facto leader of the party! And when it comes to what the party wants vs. what a legislator's constituents want, the party bosses win almost all the time. I've seen it happen with depressing regularity, and if you've been watching closely, so have you.

Writing the book helped to crystalize my thinking, but I had already decided that both clubs in my state were run by rascals and con men and that we needed more choice. I went around to grassroots groups encouraging them to run people as independents for seats in the state legislature. After all, why did we need our state representatives vetted by a private political club headquartered a thousand miles away in the D.C. cesspool? We could gather voter signatures and get on the ballot as independents. One grassroots group in particular, Secure Arkansas, took it to heart, and in early 2012 eleven people filed for seats in the state legislature as independents, which was widely regarded as the most ever. Not all were able to then go out and get the petition signatures needed to make the ballot, but seven did.

Was I one of the eleven? Yes, but we didn't know that until the night before the last full day of filing. Melissa and I watched a show together, I think it was "Psych", and the theme was "take a leap." After it was over, I looked at her and said "Should we drive to Little Rock tomorrow and file for the State House?" She said, "Sure, let's take a leap." So that's what we did.

Of course, just because I filed didn't mean I was on the ballot. I needed hundreds of voters in the district to sign a petition saying that they wanted me on the ballot. And I made a good start of it too. Because the voters had to be in the district, you couldn't just show up at the mall and sign anyone. The best way to do it was to go door-to-door. But people were mostly home between 5:30 and dark, so I got maybe two hours a day to work that, except on Saturdays. Then I got the call for that Texas project. It was actually a really good situation for me, or so I thought. I could stay with my aunt in San Antonio for a pittance and keep most of my per diem money. So, I put down my clipboard and away I went to San Antonio, figuring that it was not meant to be.

It was at that point that my wife, with a surprising strength of will for someone who is not that political, picked up the clipboard and went door-to-door and got the rest of the signatures, drove them to Little Rock and said, "Here are the signatures Mark Moore needs to get on the ballot." So that is how I got on the November of 2012 ballot as an Independent candidate for the Arkansas House of Representatives. It was almost like it wasn't even my doing. Heck, I was still in Texas, and I would stay in Texas until August 15th. When I got back there was scarcely more than two months left until early voting started!

I intended to try and win, but I started with a "relaxed" attitude toward the race, facing up to the realities of the situation. I had no "base" in the district. My family and long-time friends were elsewhere. Even my few years teaching school there were turbulent. I did make some friends among some of the students and their parents but by a quirk most of them lived on the other side of the district line. And I had basically two months to campaign, and of course way less money, though I was surprised at how much I was able to raise and I was always good at stretching a dollar.

But I had some friends who wouldn't let it go. I wasn't showing up on their doorstep begging them to campaign for me, they were showing up on mine saying, "Let's go knock on doors." They swept me up in their enthusiasm. It should have been the other way around, but the Kellers were inspiring to me as the candidate, and that was a half-dozen super-workers right there. My friend Brennan poured his usual energy into the situation, forcing me to try and keep up without notable success. My buddy Jay Fletcher had good contacts in the local community even though he lived outside the district. Heck all of them did.

My Republican opponent figured she had it in the bag until then. She didn't fill out the Family Council's voter guide questions. She didn't fill out the questions of a local Tea-Party-like group up there called "Conservative Arkansas" either. I dutifully filled out every voter guide I got, even before I got back to Arkansas. That doesn't always make a difference, but it did with the local grassroots group. They endorsed me.

I had a falling out with them after the election because I warned them that Republican Legislators would flatter them and cozy up to them just because they had endorsed an Independent. Once they were safely back on the reservation, those politicos could discount them. The ladies who ran the group chose not to listen. It turned out they were too close to a couple of the legislators- men who left office under a cloud, and one of whom is now serving a long prison term for corruption charges. It was a shame. You see it coming, you tell people it is coming, they acknowledge it is coming, and then when it comes, they do exactly what you warned them against. But it caused a stir at the time that they would endorse anyone but a Republican.

The situation with the Family Council was a lot rockier but did not end in acrimony. I answered their questionnaire by the deadline and my opponent did not. It was too late for my opponent to get her answers on the printed scorecard. Still, in the internet age many if not most people just use the web version. So, she asked for and received permission to submit her answers not only well after the deadline but also after viewing my answers online!

You may think that I called them up and complained like a crybaby. Nope. I was even sorrier than that. I drove three and a half hours to Little Rock and showed up unannounced on the doorstep of the Family Council and demanded to speak to the boss. The young man who was running the place was actually a friend of my brother-in-law and he was the kind of guy it was hard to stay mad at.

Besides that, whether it was her actual beliefs or whether she misunderstood the question, my opponent gave an unbelievably bone-headed answer. The question was something like "Do you support Obamacare's provision to use taxpayer money to pay for abortion?" That may not have been the exact question, but it was that kind of a no-brainer, particularly in a district that conservative. I mean, even people who support abortion can at least admit they don't want taxpayers to have to fund something that is widely considered abhorrent. So even though she was granted special privileges, it sort of backfired on her.

I started to get some positive press and began to think that I had a chance after all. I kept hearing that she was telling stories about me concerning the way I things ended at Pea Ridge Schools. If that was true, she never said anything about it in public, so I couldn't counterpunch. She was pretty cunning, and campaigned aggressively once she figured out that she was in a race. She focused on

Pea Ridge a lot. I guess they thought that I had a bigger base there than I did.

Another thing that made me wonder if they thought I had a bigger base there than I really did is that the Republican-controlled Benton County Election Commission greatly restricted the number of voting machines in Pea Ridge on election day. The voters were lined up for hundreds of yards. My wife and I were both ill on election night. She insisted on standing in line for four hours in order to cast a vote for me, even though we had obtained poll results and by then knew that I wasn't going to win. I couldn't holler about it if I had wanted to, because by the end of it I had lost my voice and could hardly make myself heard.

We did better in Pea Ridge than elsewhere, getting into the forties percentage-wise, but we lost the race with 38.5% of the vote overall. That sounds like a big loss, but considering the circumstances it sent shock waves through some political circles. Independent candidates were supposed to be "fringe", not grab a higher percentage of the vote than Republican candidates themselves had been getting fifteen years before. And if I had been there campaigning all Summer, I might have screwed up and won, which as it turned out would have cost my family a lot of money considering my income since that time in the private sector.

One of the seven independent candidates for the legislature even did slightly better than I did. What it showed us was that for fairly local offices like the State Legislature, being an independent didn't really hurt you if you had a good candidate. I think a couple of the ones that ran as independents and did poorly tried to run on a major party ticket before that and they also didn't do well. So, if you were a bad candidate, being an independent didn't help you, but if you were a good candidate it didn't hurt you much either. Overall, we were encouraged and thought that we would get back to our real lives and in 2014 try the same thing only bigger.

What we discovered when we turned our attention back to the project over a year later is that the Arkansas legislature responded to our actions. Reality was sending them a message. The message was that many voters were unhappy with the job they were doing and were willing to consider other options with their vote. How do you think they responded to this discordant feedback from reality? Do you think they concluded that their behavior was the problem and to fix it they should start listening to the people who elected them more and the corporate-owned party bosses less?

I was joking. Of course not. They concluded that the problem was that people still had the ability to go around them and get on the ballot as independents! Their "solution" was, among other things to make it harder to get on the ballot as an independent by changing the date by which candidates running as independents had to submit their petition signatures. Instead of filing for office with the party candidates in late February and then collecting signatures until May 1st (while party candidates with a primary opponent were in a primary contest), would-be independent candidates now had to bring their signatures with them when they filed in late February or sometimes the first two or three days of March.

In other words, what I did in 2012, decide during the filing period to run for the state legislature as an independent, was now illegal. I couldn't do like the party candidates and decide at the last minute to file by writing a check. I had to go collect signatures during the cold-weather, early-dark months of December, January, and February. I had to lay my cards on the table first, and then the establishment party guys could decide how much to bet!

Did I mention that over the past few decades, the legislature had lost several lawsuits over this exact same issue? Moving the date any earlier than May 1st had already been repeatedly ruled unconstitutional. Legislatures can't jack with election laws just to reduce their competition. There has to be a compelling state interest to make ballot access more difficult, and protecting the privileged position of the two private clubs called the "Republican" and "Democrat" parties doesn't meet that standard. They seem to think that what is good for them is good for the state, but the courts have seen it differently.

There was a fellow named Jim Lendell who was a far-left tree-hugging hippie. About the opposite kind of person from me, but in my book, he's a hero. He is the one who fought the state on this before and got the rulings that I would use to fight the state when I sued them over this change in the ballot access laws. One thing that did not survive my political battles was my narrow preconceptions about who the good guys are and who the bad guys are. There is who I agree with on policy questions and then there is who I agree with on what I would call "integrity of the process" questions. And the two groups had very little correlation!

Some people that I mostly agreed with on policy had little regard for integrity of the process issues, they just wanted those policies implemented any way they could. It was about winning. I think that is ultimately self-defeating, for everyone but especially if you claim to be a limited-government type of person. How you do things is often just as important as what you do. I found plenty of people on the old left, classical liberals, who cared about integrity of the process questions and we were united on those issues regardless of policy questions. Some on the right, often the most fearful even when they showed a lot of bravado, when it came right down to it if a rule would help what they saw as "their team" they would be for it even if it was manifestly unfair. The left has that type too, though their fears tend to be somewhat different.

I saw this play out about this time because an Independent did win a County Office about that time. The person who won ran in part on it being a non-partisan position. He was obviously the most qualified candidate, and enough voters recognized that so that he was victorious. Later, the local Republicans feted him and recruited him.

But the Republicans were not just offering carrots. They had a stick too. When it came time for him to collect signatures to run for re-election as an independent his campaign manager called me with a problem. It turns out that the official form on the Secretary of State's website for Independent candidates had been changed three days after the signature collection period for independent candidates had begun. One of the new rules the legislature had passed to jack with independents was that they had to sign an affidavit saying that all of their signatures were collected properly and on the correct form. In those three days this campaign had already collected hundreds of signatures on the old form. When this fellow contacted the Secretary of State's Office about it, no one there would put it in writing that it was OK to use the previous form! They just expressed verbally that they thought it would be OK. This was what he explained to me.

The campaign first decided that they had to start over. Then there was the question of how to weed out the old forms, since they looked much the same. A few weeks later, the campaign manager called me back. He said that this was his candidate's way to make a living, and they couldn't risk not making the ballot on some contrived technicality. He was going to accept the Republican's offer to be their candidate. I told them that he was joining himself to people that he knows operate as thugs. I don't think he took it personally, because in his heart he agreed!

Chapter Twelve

I Sue the State

Obviously, independents were going to be "out of the game" for a while. And people who engage in political action hate being out of the game! The small band of great folks that I had managed to gather in order to promote people running as independents drifted away. Soon it was down to me and Tom Mayfield.

Well, OK that was skipping ahead some. Before that point, I got a phone call from Tom. On paper, Tom was still the point of contact for the Constitution Party of Arkansas. He had already figured out they weren't the answer, but he hadn't found anyone to hand it over to. He said that he had been contacted by an attorney from Tulsa named Jim Linger. Mr. Linger told him that the state's recently passed laws for ballot access for new parties was unconstitutional. He was interested in finding a party to sue the state and get the laws overturned.

Well, it was true about the laws for new parties, the legislature was clamping down on all ways around the two establishment parties by passing restrictions that had already been declared unconstitutional. But the new laws for independent candidates that were unconstitutional was what I was interested in at the moment.

Tom put me together with Mr. Linger and we went over the facts of the case. The same early deadline had been declared unconstitutional by federal courts on two or three occasions, and here they were doing it again. Once he checked into it, Mr. Linger agreed to take the case. Not for free though. He wanted a deposit of $3500 up front. Everything else, he would count on the court to rule in our favor and then pay him out of a civil rights fund that is ultimately taken from the state. I didn't realize this at the time, but when a state loses a civil rights case the judge can rule that the state must pay the plaintiff's lawyers.

Mr. Linger wound up taking the case with only $1,750 from Arkansas Neighbors (most of it mine) in retainer. He was a long-time specialist in ballot access law and looking at the case history he felt the evidence was overwhelmingly in our favor. In fact, early on he opined that the state would take a look at the evidence from his brief and just fold. He knew the law, but I knew the state Republican Party. I told him that they would fight to the last taxpayer dollar in order to defend rules that they believed helped screen their party from competition, no matter how blatantly unconstitutional.

Mr. Linger told me that to be plaintiffs, it would be best if we went down during the filing period and filed for public office. That way we could ask for standing in the case both as voters and as potential candidates. He correctly anticipated that they would lean heavily on an argument of "standing". That is, they would claim that it didn't matter whether what they were doing was wrong or not, because I didn't even have a right to question it in a court of law. They would claim that I lacked "standing" to pursue the case.

Mr. Linger suggested that one of us run for a statewide office. Looking over the offices, I decided to file for Lt. Governor. If for some reason I was wrong and the state folded quickly, I could be on the ballot, and I figured why run for an office which costs millions to be a competitive candidate? Former Congressman Tim Griffin was expected to win the Republican nomination, and the only Democrat who wanted to run wasn't considered a strong candidate. In my mind, Griffin had worked his way up as a system-guy, and an oppo-research shark for guys like Karl Rove.

I don't want to say that I didn't think he had earned it, but he was the guy I wanted to run against. When working for Rove he was implicated in voter suppression when an email from his account was accidentally sent to a journalist fishing for data. The title of the email was "Voter caging" and attached was a list of minority voters in Florida. The idea seemed to be that they would send them all a card and then see which ones came back "not at this address" and then challenge their voter registration. Say some black kid signed up for the Navy and was on an eighteen-month deployment? So what if his lease at his apartment where he registered lapsed? Should he get his vote tossed just because he was targeted based on his color?

How he lived that one down is a testament to how protected some connected guys are. The press keeps coming to him and lobbing him softballs but they never seemed to get around to reporting on that, or if they did it was kind of dismissive, not reporting while bug-eyed with nostrils flaring like they would if it was someone they were targeting.

If I had to guess, and it is just a guess not even rising to the level of a theory, Griffin was covering for Rove. It is well known that Rove didn't have his own email. He used other people's email accounts to send messages. That way it was hard to trace things back to him and he always had an intermediary to take the fall. Maybe Rove was the one who messed up and sent his dirty tricks message to a journalist by mistake. My hypothesis is that Griffin "took one for the team" and in exchange strings were pulled so that the media gave him kid gloves treatment. It is just a hypothesis, and I may never know, but it does connect a few dots.

There is another wrinkle to all of this. Remember the young state legislator that buddied up to me after he thought I put an independent up against him? The one that became a sincere ally in several battles? Well, he was now the Secretary of State, the person that I would have to sue to challenge the law. The Republican establishment in the state hadn't particularly backed him. He just ran a good campaign for a lower-profile office and had the same name as a famous race-car driver from Jonesboro. He managed to win by a small margin and was for a time the only Republican statewide office holder in Arkansas State government.

I had spent the last few years being one of his strongest defenders in the state. The media launched one unfair attack after another on him from the moment he took the oath of office. The Democrat incumbent didn't exactly provide him with a sporting turnover. When he walked in the door, he found paper shredders parked in the middle of the office, bins packed to the gills with the shreds of all of the organizational flowcharts and job descriptions. He had no idea who was responsible for what, and had no way of finding out except by asking the staff hired by his predecessor in the other party. So about the first thing he did was take his new hires and the old hires on a team-building exercise in northwest Arkansas. They acted like he was wasting taxpayer money.

That was just one small sample. As near as I could tell, those first few years the state media simply did not know how to tell the truth about Mark Martin. There was seldom a point of intersection where what they wrote about Mark Martin was what was happening in the real world. I wrote blog posts defending him, which was about like a pea-shooter going up against a howitzer. His "colleagues" in the Republican party ran and hid, lest they run afoul of the pressmasters. While he got savaged time after time with easily refutable lies, his so-called party could not even be bothered to put up a press release on their website in his defense. People had to come to my blog for that! This was the guy I was going to have to sue, even though my real beef was with the legislature.

Mark Martin was a team player for his party, but they never really reciprocated. I have a theory as to why. Remember my friend John Barry Baker who figured out what it meant to be an insider? "When the chips are down you have to be willing to do the wrong thing for the right people." They couldn't trust Mark Martin to do that. He did a lot I didn't like, but he had a moral core and they could never tell when or if that would get in the way of party business. So they left him to twist in the wind even when he was the only statewide Republican office-holder in Arkansas State government.

The first couple of years I thought that I was suing him in his professional capacity. I was naïve about the details of the process. It turned out that this would violate the "sovereign immunity" of the state government if state officials could be sued in federal court. So they came up with this legal doctrine whereby people could sue office holders as private persons for the way they acted in their state capacity.

Actually, that whole thing sounds shady to me. It sounds like an end-run around the constitution's provision on "sovereign immunity." I doubt that I would have even sought out the suit if I had understood that going in. I originally figured that Congress had authority under the 14th Amendment to make laws applicable to the states concerning equality under the law and that they had passed some law to which this suit applied. Later I figured out this didn't happen and a lot of this was judge-created "law."

So for the first couple of years of this I was conflicted about even having to sue Martin. The last few years there was this added burden. I had (and have) serious doubts about the whole legal theory under which it was done. Though if it should apply anywhere, it should be ballot access. That is because making the rules under which there should be competition for their own jobs is the one thing that they should not be sovereign about!

Anyway, I think I drove Mr. Linger nuts pestering him to call and see why we didn't have a court date and to get this thing moving. Probably mostly to put me off, he suggested I commission a poll to see if there was any support for a new candidate for Lt. Governor at this stage of the game. Somehow, I managed to get the data and a firm to run the poll. It was as I suspected, a month or two before the election most of the voters had no idea who the candidates for Lt. Governor of Arkansas were, and at least a fifth were willing to vote for an independent.

It didn't help. The first trial did not take place until way after the election. Mark Martin just turned the case over to his Deputy, A.J. Kelley, and after that basically did not involve himself. A.J. Kelley had a legal style that was designed to discourage people from suing the Secretary of State. That is, if someone sued his office, he had a habit of "challenging everything" and doing anything he could think of to drag it out and delay. Maybe they were waiting for me to die or run out of money? The state kept making demands and filings and basically raising every issue they could think of. If it was an issue they didn't care about it might have been different, but this was a law passed by his fellow Republicans in the legislature and they were going to fight it to the last taxpayer dollar, just as I predicted.

I can see their side of it, if they had a duty to uphold the law then even if the legislature passed a stupid law, they were supposed to fight for it. On the other hand, they also had a duty to uphold the constitution, and this same provision had already been declared unconstitutional several times. The legislature put the Secretary of State in a difficult position by passing such blatantly unconstitutional laws. But the way they resolved the conflict was to pretend that there wasn't a conflict. I like to think that if I had been on the other side then I would have balanced the need to uphold the law with the need to follow the constitution. At some point you have to appeal to the well-established legal principle that a law which is unconstitutional isn't a law at all. I would not have backed the legislature to the hilt for what was plainly an attempt to place an unnecessary barrier to ballot access for citizens who don't wish to join their partisan club. At the very least, I would not have fought for five years to try to prevent a ruling from even taking place. I would have asked for the ruling to end the conflict. But that isn't going to happen when both branches are buddies in the same political club, and that's just another reason why I think we need a lot more independents in office.

After the election, both we and the state put forth motions for "Summary Judgement". That is, we both thought that it should not have to go to a full trial because our case was so overwhelming and the facts were not in dispute. Our document was maybe a dozen pages long. The "brief" filed by the state was ten times that length!

To give you some perspective about how ridiculously long that is, when Sidney Powell alleged that there was a vast conspiracy to rig the Presidential Election in Georgia, she laid out her claims and evidence in a "brief" that was 104 pages in length. The one the state filed in our case was longer than the one she filed for a case that big! If you added our brief onto hers, it still wouldn't be as long as the brief the state filed raising any claim they could think of. A.J. Kelley threw everything but the kitchen sink at us, whether the accusation could be well-supported or not. Basically, he just threw everything up against the wall hoping something would stick. He was playing his weak hand the best it could be played. If you don't have any good reasons for the court to rule in your favor, offer up a bunch of bad reasons and hope one of them gets through!

His favorite argument was an argument that I did not have "standing". That is, regardless of the merits of our case or whether the law was right or wrong, I had no right to even be there asking the court to consider it. His position was that I should have collected the fifteen thousand signatures I would have needed for ballot access and then ask the judge if it was OK to turn them in late.

I wanted a ruling on the law before I tried something that hard and that expensive to do.

As I mentioned earlier, this whole experience deeply affected my formerly narrow ideas about who the "good guys" are and who the "bad guys" are. Some people that I might agree with on public policy, I totally disagreed with on "integrity of the process" issues. They may or may not care if the way something was done was fair and proper or not, so long as their desired policy was enacted. I thought that if it wasn't done in an above-board manner it shouldn't be done. The end does not justify the means, rather the use of unfair means will corrupt those resorting to them so that their ends turn out bad too. I met people who I would not agree with at all on some very important issues, but they were with me in this fight when almost all of my ideological friends had no regard for it at all.

Layered on top of that is my old-school Christian belief that we are all the "bad guys" and need to constantly check our hearts and motives, with frequent repentance. Jesus Christ is the only real "good guy" and the rest of us, me, my allies and my enemies, are bound by sin and in need of cleansing. I realize that isn't the view of the distortion of Christianity which has taken over many Christian churches, especially those whose parishioners are politically active. The warped theology predominant in our day is that both sides hire spiritual leaders who assure them that they are the "good guys" and their enemies are the "bad guys". They are trying to sign God up on their team to bring wrath on the evil-doers. If He did, would any of us be standing?

Fortunately for us, in classic Christian theology the punishment for our misdeeds is dealt with, not rationalized away or projected onto our political enemies, through the sacrifice of God the Son. So salvation comes from seeing how good He is, not how awesome we are. It doesn't come from faith in ourselves that we are the "good guys". Rather the salvation He provides can be accessed only once we realize that we are also the "bad guys" and in need of Him!

The toxic twisting of the Christian faith that we see from both left and right has politicians trying to muscle into the seat of Christ, where they are "the Lord's Anointed" and therefore if you oppose what they have done, you are automatically opposing God! Instead, we should all scrutinize each other closely, realizing that all of us fall short. It is the only healthy way to do it, but also one that the sin nature of man hates. We just want to root for our team or champion without that kind of reflection that helps keep us all on the straight and narrow path.

I have a reason for that religious rabbit-trail. During the five years of this case, my priorities of life shifted. I began to see the problem even more as a spiritual one and less as a political one. Marianne Williamson may be someone I consider flakey, but when she said "We are not going to policy-wonk our way out of this" she was onto something. People who are warped by greed or fear or reckless hate or any other bad thing are not, in the long run, going to be well governed. Our needs went beyond getting a new batch of political leaders, we needed spiritual renewal.

About this time, I started reading the early part of the book of Genesis from the Bible and I started seeing things in there that I had never noticed before. It is probably the most maligned part of scripture, but I started seeing it in a very profound way. After that point I spent what little free time I had writing and rewriting and honing a four-hundred-page book on early Genesis called "Early Genesis, the Revealed Cosmology." I am sure that some of you reading this have long since dismissed the book of Genesis as nonsense. A lot of claims about what the text is saying are nonsense, but there is a lot of "theology that isn't really in the Bible" going on there.

At any rate, I am not going to try and change anyone's mind about that here, I am just describing how my priorities changed. It wasn't that I did not care for politics anymore, but only within the context of a higher calling. Politics is very seductive and I have seen it a lot the other way, with the political tail wagging the spiritual dog. God isn't going to be a means to any other end. He won't bless it. At any rate, let me get back to my adventures in suing the state.

The main person I met that volunteered to help with the case was a man from San Francisco, California, Richard Winger. He had put out a newsletter for decades called "Ballot Access News". This man was independently wealthy. He could have done whatever he wanted to do with his life. He chose to spend it helping people from outside the establishment parties get ballot access. He became the foremost expert on American ballot access law in the world. When my attorney wanted the background on ballot access cases in Arkansas, he went to Richard Winger. When we wanted a ruling from an obscure ballot access case that was unavailable in any public record, we went to Richard Winger. His knowledge of these cases was encyclopedic. His house had all kinds of such records. He was our "Expert Witness" in the case.

I doubt that Richard Winger is a Christian. We probably don't share many of the same views on public policy outside of ballot access questions. We live very different lives. That did not stop him from investing a lot of personal time and energy helping us on this case. He did it for all kinds of people, for free. And he has been doing it for decades. A true life of public service. After we met him, my wife suggested that a documentary about his life's work would be something worth watching. That was the seed of the idea for the documentary which eventually became "Access". Since we didn't have the budget and resources to travel all over the country talking to the people he helped, in practical terms we wound up talking about our own struggles with Richard's story folded into it. But the project started out as a tribute to his life's work. The original working title was "Ballot Access News", the name of his newsletter.

The circuit court agreed that I had standing from the git-go, even as just a voter I had standing, but I also had standing as a candidate. I should not have had to go to such trouble and expense just to find

Journey on the Outside

out if I coul... ...enge the law! Mr. Kelley appealed that decision on be... he state and it went to the Eighth Circuit. A three-judge... concurred that I had standing.

I will ski... ...ad on this part to show you how determined they were not to let go on this. Kelley tried to appeal it to the U.S. Supreme Court, but they refused to even hear him. It did cost me another $700 to have a brief printed up just in case they did though. Eventually, after many motions and delays, the case was kicked back down to the district court where the state once again raised the same issue that had already been shot down. It was shot down again, and they appealed and went to another three-judge panel from the Eighth Circuit and tried to argue the same thing yet again.

Lest you think this was just A.J. Kelley being some kind of fanatic, when Martin was term-limited out and his successor John Thurston came in, he got new counsel, Michael Fincher. That guy made A.J. look like a sweetheart. The administration changed (though they were both Republicans) but the policy of unrelenting opposition at all costs didn't change. It only got worse. I think because I had no personal relationship with anyone in the new regime to mitigate the "take no prisoners" mentality that was everywhere in party politics.

Heck all the Thurston regime had left to argue about whether the state was going to get stuck with the bill for my lawyer. Despite that, they *still* tried to argue standing when that had already been decided four times and had nothing to do with the issue of who should pay the bills. It was unbelievable. They also made some very personal accusations about both me and my attorney, but I am skipping ahead in the story.

As I mentioned, A.J. Kelley seemed to be of the opinion that the best way to minimize the number of suits that the State was subjected to was to make anyone who sued the state have to answer a slew of counter-accusations and do a pile of work on every issue related to the case. That was his style anyway, and it was accentuated in this case by the fact that he didn't have a good argument. His solution to this problem was to make a very large number of bad arguments. It was a "throw everything against the wall and see if something sticks" approach. It tied right into his strategy of wearing people out who tried to sue the state.

The judge was a rookie federal judge, James Moody Jr., with a distinguished pedigree since his father was also a federal judge. At the request for summary judgement, he agreed with all of our arguments and only one of theirs. They had submitted an affidavit saying that, due to changes in the law, they just couldn't process the petition signatures after May 1st and therefore even if it was a serious burden on citizens seeking office as independents it was now "necessary". At this juncture, the rookie federal judge tended to take the state at its word. By the end of this case five years later, he was totally onto them. But initially he ruled that even though we were right in everything we were saying and we had standing, the state was compelled by "necessity" to move up the petition deadline.

My attorney, Jim Linger of Tulsa, appealed on the grounds that they had not proven their claim that it was "necessary" to demand the petitions earlier. All we had was an affidavit from someone in the Secretary of State's office with no opportunity to question or examine the claim. We wouldn't ever get one either, at least with the fellow who signed the affidavit. Shortly thereafter he was abruptly gone from the Secretary of State's office and to this day I don't know why.

After many delays and motions and maneuvers, which took years, we got in front of the Eighth Circuit's Three Judge Panel. Since Judge Moody had agreed with us on every other issue, the only thing for us to argue about was whether there was a question of fact in dispute (whether it was true that it was now "necessary" that the state move the petition submissions forward), and therefore the judge should not have given the state a summary judgement in its favor.

Judge LaVinsky Smith was the head of the Eighth Circuit, and probably the sharpest of the bunch. He ruled that there was a question of fact in dispute, and that the state had a chance to provide evidence for it and had failed to do so (an affidavit making a bald assertion didn't count for much). He voted not only to void the Summary Judgement against us, but to reverse Judge Moody and award us the win right there. The other two judges opted to send the case back down to Judge Moody with specific instructions that he was to ascertain whether the state's claim was true or not, and make a new ruling after a formal trial based on that. Of course, the state was still trying to raise every issue it could, including "standing" but the panel brushed them off.

Eventually, in December of 2019, I finally got my day in court. Remember that the suit had originally been filed in February of 2014. Some would say that Justice Delayed is Justice Denied, but as you will see, it was all a part of God's good plan. Believe me I am far from bitter. It makes a much better story like this than if we had won early!

When we finally got in court, I experienced the most one-sided trial you have ever seen in your life. Linger was like Perry Mason out there, guiding even the state witness to the point where the young man admitted they could get the job done no matter when the independent signatures were submitted and that it was therefore not "necessary" for the state to move the date to turn in the petitions forward. I mean, the evidence strongly suggested that it would even be easier for the state to validate them in May, the original date we wanted, than in February. At any rate, the state needed a much higher signature validating capacity for its other functions than it needed for independent candidates. It just was not a significant burden on the state at all.

Of course, Mr. Kelley tried to make it about "standing" and everything else. Judge Moody tolerated it, probably because he didn't want to give any grounds for appeal that would stand, but the case concluded and we walked out of there thinking that when the decision dropped, usually in a matter of weeks, we would be in good shape.

Although we got word that Judge Moody would rule in our favor, the actual decision did not drop for a couple of weeks. Finally, in January, it came. It was narrowly drawn in that while it found the law unconstitutional, it extended relief to me only. It said that Mark Moore could file his paperwork to run for public office as late as noon on May 1st, rather than the March 2nd date under the original overturned law. In practical effect it meant that anyone could file then though, because my case became a precedent. Now I had to decide if I was going to file for anything. The party candidate filing period ended March 2nd. The law as written said that independents, for no good reason, had to file their intention to be a candidate with the party candidates, even if we could now collect our petition signatures afterward.

I was very conflicted. A part of me wanted to run for office, but it was time to face facts. Lt. Governor was realistically out of reach. The incumbent had played his cards well and was a much stronger candidate than he was four years ago. At some point in all of this, I also found out my old friend Frank Gilbert was the Libertarian candidate for Lt. Governor. Why not just support Frank? We were not in a financial position for me to quit my project early, which was way across the state line, and campaign full time for a state-wide office. And if I ran, I wanted more than a moral victory.

I really had no idea what to do. The more I looked at Lt. Governor the more I soured on it. I thought about running for Secretary of State. I called a friend who was a State Senator and asked for his input. He offered to back me against Griffin for Lt. Governor, but kind of liked Thurston. I was going to have to spend money, or borrow money, or beg friends for money, if I wanted to start a signature collection campaign that had any hope of success for a statewide office. It would cost probably $30,000 to get the signatures even with some volunteer help.

All of this was weighing on my mind when the week-long filing period started. I had no idea what to do, but felt like I should do something. Then the second day of the filing period came and I got a call from Mr. Linger. The state had filed another motion in our case. "What is it about?" I asked him. He said "I don't know, they don't have to tell us for two weeks. They just gave notice that they are going to file."

If I wasn't frozen enough, that did it. It just made no sense to commit to spending a bunch of money to get the signatures, whether my own or my friend's, when there was the cloud of a new motion hanging over things. Did this ever end? It had been five years already, did they have the power to drag it out past yet another election cycle, so that I would be spending the money for nothing? The filing period week came and went, and I wound up doing nothing.

Once the state revealed what was in their motion, around March 8th, I was disgusted. They had filed a motion stating that since I had not filed for office, that the ruling should be set aside as moot. Well, how did they know that? They entered the motion after only the first day of the candidate filing period, not the last! How did they know that I wasn't going to file on the last day? Heck, I didn't even know! The fact that there was an unknown motion was what made me chuck the idea of filing.

When my lead attorney, Jim Linger, called me to talk about it, I complained that their actions contributed to my failure to file. Then he went all Perry Mason on me again. He noted that the ruling said that I could file my paperwork for public office as late as noon of May 1st, it didn't specify that I had to file my candidate paperwork in the party candidate filing period that had just passed, and turn in my signatures by May 1st. It just said I had until May 1st to turn in my paperwork to file as a candidate.

The thing was, I was still in Kansas on a project. It wasn't going that well and it would end that same year anyway. The state would later hyperventilate over my admission in my affidavit that I was out of state a lot, but I was drawing per diem for my time out of state. My home was always in Arkansas. While a statewide race was out of the question, I did think long and hard about the State Senate District back home.

The lady who was our long-time State Senator was someone I had gone door-to-door for a long time ago. By this time, her husband had a high-dollar job working for the Governor. Her son also had a high-dollar job working for the Governor. Both were doctors, so it wasn't like they were unqualified men. They were good men. I just thought that she would have a hard time separating the desires of her constituents from those of the Governor. If they wanted something and he wanted something different, so much of her family income came from his patronage that it created at least the appearance of impropriety.

My experience is that those in the club never even consider that there could be a conflict of interest. Legislators just naturally take their cues from the Governor when he is of their party, no constituent input needed, or desired. They are shocked when someone points out how it looks when your family winds up with high-paying jobs in state government, while normal people look at that and instantly see it.

Anyway, I thought I'd like to file for State Senate, but how to organize a petition drive while working full time and doing right by my wife and kids? It was about that time, out of the blue, my old friend Jay Fletcher called. He asked me if I was going to run for anything. He is a salt-of-the-earth type of man who is always going on mission trips. It never occurred to him that the window for filing for public office was supposed to already be closed for that cycle.

When I explained the situation, he immediately volunteered to coordinate the campaign. He got some folks to collect signatures but also did the logistics with a couple of pros that I hired for the task.

Fact is I did not know exactly how many signatures I would need to qualify. The Secretary of State's office didn't make that information available, unless you called and asked about a specific office. At this point, relations were strained, and I was not ready to tip them off yet that we intended to file anyway, per our interpretation of the language of the ruling. Still, I had bought voter data from a couple of years before and used it to calculate my own figure. I forget the exact number but I think I calculated about 750 would get us over the hump.

The Senator called me and made her appeal to get me to not run. It turned out that a Democrat had filed too, and if the conservative vote was split, she could lose. Of course, I had been advocating for run-offs for years, preferably instant runoff voting, sometimes called "Ranked Choice Voting". If "vote-splitting" was such a problem, it was no one's fault but the Republicans and Democrats who wrote the election laws. It is a scandal that they have run-offs in their own primaries and in elections for their own party officers, but not for the general public! They force us into a "first past the post" method of determining a winner in which people are afraid to vote for a third-party candidate or independent because of vote-splitting. I figured if my candidacy did initiate a train wreck, maybe they'd finally fix it.

Then someone who was a friend of mine for years called. At one time he was like an older brother to me. I looked up to him. They were very good to me. Something happened and he and his wife basically cut me off socially. I never knew why. Out of the blue, after having not spoken to me for years he called to lobby me to get out of the race. I was hurt and offended that the first time I heard from him was under these circumstances. I didn't say all that to him. I should have but I didn't, but I also refused to leave the race.

By now the new regime was in place at the Secretary of State's office. When we went down there and filed of course they had a cow. They filed yet another motion asking the judge to clarify his order. He made it plain that I could file for any office I wanted and I did not have to turn in any papers when the party candidates filed back in February, I could do it all on May 1st.

This marked a dramatic turning point in sixty years of struggle over fair ballot access for independent candidates in Arkansas. For decades the powers that be in the state- it didn't matter which establishment party was in power, they behaved in an identical manner- had played this game. They would pass an unconstitutional law restricting access to the ballot for any group other than themselves, and then when they finally got sued over it and lost in court they would grudgingly change the law.....until the judges were not looking. Then they would put the unconstitutional hurdles to ballot access back in place. Frequently, the very same provisions that were specifically declared unconstitutional would be reinstated after a few years. Activists would then have to go back to court to reverse the very same restrictions that had already been thrown out on previous occasions.

The reason for this outrageous and unprincipled behavior was two-fold. One was the fact that political parties tend to bring out the worst in people and they really do start thinking that what is good for their political club is good for the Republic. Morality is redefined and seen in terms of what is good for their team. Once they get to this point, they can act with the full approval of their conscience. They really can't see how wrong it is, because it isn't wrong if it helps their team! That is a big reason why I believe in independent candidates and multiple parties that can rise and fall in response to events rather than two entrenched institutional parties that people are emotionally invested in to the point where it jacks with both their reason and their morality.

The second reason is that once this degradation in moral fiber is advanced the only thing restraining people from evil is the prospect of deterrence, and there was no deterrence. The only thing that happened to them is that after a few years of court battles they would be forced to give back what they took and change the law back to what it had been before. Imagine some group convinced themselves that taking your stuff was OK if it was good for their team. Then the only "punishment" they got if caught with your stuff is that they had to give back your stuff until they had the next chance to take it. There was no deterrent. Sure, they often had to pay for the plaintiff's attorneys but even then, it wasn't their personal dollars, it wasn't dollars from their political party. It was only taxpayer dollars that were being used to drag these suits out.

Even though in their minds they were good stewards of taxpayer money and against government waste, it just never occurred to them that using taxpayer money to keep the competition down was a bad thing. Why of course it was a good use of taxpayer money, it was helping their political party!

But sixty years of this kind of game got upended once Judge Moody ruled that I could both file and turn in my petition signatures by May 1st. They had always made independent candidates file with the party candidates. We didn't even challenge them on that in our initial suit, though it was obviously another needless hassle. There was no reason to make independent candidates file their paperwork with the party candidates, we were not going to be in a primary election.

If this case stood, his ruling on this issue would become precedent. The next go-around someone could sue them on the early filing period for independents and have an excellent chance to win. Suddenly independents would have an "advantage" of not being forced to file with the party candidates. For the first time in sixty years the rules of the game changed. Instead of just being forced to give back what they took, they were facing the prospect of having to give up something else in addition to what they took!

By then the new administration had taken over, but it was the same party and the same mindset. I am sure it would be the same mindset if the other establishment party had won, but Arkansas at this point was a one-party state. Nothing changed, unless it got worse. Even though this outcome was 100% the result of their over-aggressive efforts backfiring on them, they wanted the decision, the whole decision, stricken from the record and ruled moot.

The State appealed again to the Eighth Circuit, basically saying since the legislature had been such good boys and changed the law back to what it was, the case was moot. The legislature was quick to comply, but I wonder if a part of their promptness wasn't based on the realization that this time, for the first time, they had some chips to lose if the ruling stood?

Part of their argument was that I did not get enough good signatures to qualify for that State Senate race. I thought I did, we turned in what we thought were more than enough signatures to qualify. The thing is, my voter list did not include voters who had voted in the previous election but then moved off, so my 3% of the voters was a smaller number than the actual 3%. I still turned in a little over the true number, but they were easily able to find enough bad signatures to keep me off the ballot. Still, I made a good-faith effort and it was sort of like running in a primary and losing, I was still a legitimate candidate. Not that their appeal conceded any of that.

Well, they appealed to the Eighth Circuit and we got another three-judge panel. One of them bought into the state's arguments. He said if it happens again, the remedy would be for us to do this all over again. He said that like it hadn't taken us five years of fighting and many dollars out of my own pocket to get here. The other two judges were more on the ball. They "got it". The fact that Judge Moody's ruling allowed me to file after the filing period for party candidates was raised by the state as a reason the decision should be thrown out as moot. The Circuit Judges asked what was so bad about that? They also couldn't see why a non-party candidate should have to file with the party candidates. "By tradition, independents file with the party candidates" was the best that the state could do. One judge was not fooled for an instant. "By tradition? You mean you make them." He replied.

Ultimately, the Circuit Court ruled 2-1 that the decision would stand. In their ruling, they noted that independents had successfully sued Arkansas over ballot access law on many occasions in the past, and that because of this history, it was in the public interest that there be a large body of precedent on this issue. They wanted this "guidance" to the state legislature to stay on the record!

I looked at it as a very tactful way of saying that the court had about had it with Republicans and Democrats in Arkansas jerking people around by passing and re-passing ballot access laws that any fool could tell had already been ruled unconstitutional. I found it particularly interesting that the issue of the relaxed filing period had been raised and was brushed off by the court as a reason to moot the case, and that they then specifically ruled that the case should stand and become precedent. The state was now exposed to another lawsuit unless they willingly loosened the requirements for the filing period of independent candidates. Was the state chastened? Hardly. After that, Secretary of State Thurston's office got unbelievably ugly about the whole thing.

You might wonder what there was left to fight about? The only valid issue remaining was whether or not the state should pay my attorney's fees. My attorney was very circumspect in what he asked for. Nevertheless, Thurston's office, through his attorney Michael Fincher, filed an objection that was really over the top. And they tried to reargue the whole case again, not just talk about the issue at hand, which was payment of attorney fees. Some samples of the ugly from their filing:

"The facts of this case show that it is a sham, and fraud upon this court." They wrote. And further, "Moore received relief through deception." They went on to say that they had doubts about my veracity and "Moore's change of position was not a good-faith mistake." They said "Moore's deliberate actions throughout the case created numerous complications" as if it wasn't the Secretary of State's office that was dragging the thing out for five years by raising every imaginable objection and trying to take standing all the way to the Supreme Court and back.

Thurston's lawyer argued for "Estoppel" because it was appropriate when "a party abuses the judicial forum or process by making a knowing misrepresentation or perpetrating a fraud on the court." In his mind, I was that offending party. In fact, in the pleading which was strictly over the question of who should pay attorney's fees, the new administration was *still* trying to argue standing! They were very angry that a mere common citizen was able to persevere and even prevail against them. Who the heck did I think I was?

They even insulted my attorney, Mr. Linger, who beat them like a rug in springtime. They argued that the courts should not pay him the normal rate of an out-of-town lawyer because the fact that I had local counsel as well proved that local counsel was available to do the work. Meanwhile they argued that the local lawyer should not be paid anything because Mr. Linger did all the work! The incongruency of these accusations never seemed to dawn on them.

They also questioned his expertise. After all the state did to drag this out for years and raise every possible objection, they had the nerve to say, "It did not take any expertise to file "shot-gun pleadings", and the fact that the case wasn't amended, but saved through inappropriate affidavits in responsive pleadings argues heavily against expertise." Sounds like a powerful case of projection to me.

What really happened was that the over-aggressive tactics of the state backfired against them. The reason we could file a "responsive pleading" was that they were always launching new motions for us to respond to. As it is written in the scripture, "He who digs a pit will fall into it." That is, they will fall into the traps they set for others. So it was here. Their motions allowed us to respond, and we responded effectively. Their complaint was kind of like someone objecting that the person they are throwing punches at is good at ducking and counter-punching! It took a lot of nerve to imply that my attorney Jim Linger, who beat them despite all the resistance that the state could muster, lacked expertise.

Of course, most of this legal battle occurred during the previous administration, but this was the same political team (team Red) and the unrelenting and implacable opposition to restoring the ballot access law to its prior, constitutional, form did not change with the administration. The only thing that changed was that the state was much uglier and more personal in their attacks once the Thurston Regime took over. When Mark Martin was the Secretary of State, he didn't even keep track of the case, he just turned it over to A.J. Kelley. And while Kelley was a bit pull and had a philosophy of contesting everything, it wasn't *personal*. This was personal.

Judge Moody didn't fit the role of a judicial activist. He wasn't trying to become a voting-rights civil-liberties champion. He just wanted to impartially apply the law. If anything, his initial instincts were to defer to the state. But it seems that this filing was just too much. In his decision awarding Mr. Linger over $54,000 he wrote "In addition, the Secretary reargues the merits of the case and makes a slew of baseless allegations that Plaintiff lacked veracity throughout the litigation, that Plaintiff abused the judicial forum, and that Plaintiff's counsel lacked expertise which resulted in 'shotgun pleadings.' These arguments are completely without merit."

It was unusually blunt talk from a federal judge. In the ruling he was very complimentary of Mr. Linger's expertise, which clearly exceeded the state's! The judge ruled that the state had to pay Mr. Linger $54,000 in attorney's fees. The only thing he didn't agree with us on was awarding our local attorney, Jeff Rosenzweig, attorney's fees as well. Judge Moody felt it was duplicative since Mr. Linger was the go-to guy on basically everything. I felt bad about Jeff getting shut out. I told Mr. Linger he could keep my pitiful little deposit, with an eye to it going to him.

Chapter Thirteen

ACCESS

My wife and I looked back on the effort that we had to make just for us to challenge the state on one tiny corner of injustice. We try to learn from everything we go through together. Even though she is much less into politics than I am, she never wavered on our commitment to that battle. This was the case even though we had a lean year in there where we wondered where the next month's utility bills were going to come from. The experience was one of the defining ones of my adult life.

As we discussed it, we decided that we had more than a court victory, we had a good story to tell. Not just our story, but the state government had been passing laws making it hard for new parties to get on the ballot too, and those people had a story to tell. And this issue was not limited to our state. Meeting Richard Winger was eye-opening on many levels. A lot of people like to talk about how unselfish they are, and how they are running for office because they want to help others, but this guy was living it, with no thought or expectation of any reward. He had the money to do what he wanted with his life, and what he spent it on was helping others with obscure, anti-establishment ideas, get a fair shake on ballot access. He was helping the "losers" of the process, the ones that the movers and shakers found to be an irritant if they thought of them at all. And he did this for free whether people believed in his overall political positions or not. He wanted to help the "outcasts".

Melissa pointed out that this would make a great story for a documentary. She was the one who proposed that someone make a documentary about Richard Winger and his lifelong commitment to helping oddballs and outsiders like us get fair ballot access laws. We soon realized that we knew a young man who produced documentaries, John Erwin. We approached him with the idea of partnering with us. I knew all the players and could provide shoestring financing, and he had the gear and the experience to whip it up into an actual documentary. The provisional title was "Ballot Access News", after the newsletter that Richard had put out for decades. Later, we shortened the title to "Access".

We originally intended to interview people from several of Richard's big cases around the country, and make our story just one of the threads. We quickly figured out that our budget did not permit that. Tracking down the people from those cases would also be difficult. We'd have to use the more recent cases in Arkansas as examples of what had been going on for decades all around the country. At any rate, we had asked Richard about his more compelling cases and he said that Arkansas was probably the most blatant example of a state repeatedly pushing the same illegal ballot restrictions over and over again.

Over time the project morphed into being more about the struggle than about any one person's role in the struggle. That's probably just the way he'd like it anyway. Thanks to my years of activism, I either knew the folks involved or knew someone who did. Some of them were Libertarian. Some were far left. What I found was that it didn't matter, I connected with pretty much all of them.

Nobody joins a minor party to follow popular personalities or to enrich themselves. They do it based on ideals. They have principles. Maybe we didn't share some of the same principles but they thought and spoke like people who were motivated by ideals and principles, just like I was. From my time as a Republican, and I noticed Democrats were the same, I saw a lot of people were in it with the same mind-set that a fan would have for a sports team. They just wanted a side to cheer on in the "game". The policies were secondary, or maybe didn't really matter at all. They liked "winning" even if that didn't translate to doing any good.

People susceptible to this mind-set sometimes have a tendency to become almost like groupies. They just want to rub shoulders with politicians and feel "special". Others were there because there was something in it for them. Maybe it was just making sure that those on top now stayed on top, no matter what. I don't want to condemn those folks. There is some of that in everybody, me included. It is just that it is a primary trait in some and way down the list for others. The bottom line was that one thing which surprised me going around helping John Erwin interview all of these folks, was how well we got along. What made us tick was similar even if our conclusions often differed.

I know that establishment politicians work together to advance their interests. They wear different party hats, but the truth is, they get along far better with the insiders in the other party than they do the outsiders in their own party. Maybe us outsiders should take a page from that playbook. Maybe we should work together to get ballot access for outsider viewpoints, even if we don't share those views.

I don't know what the future holds. Maybe there will be some kind of movement I can help out with. Maybe there will be another unjust law that needs to be challenged. Maybe I will fold some of that into another run for public office. Or maybe I am done with all of that and I will spend most of my extra energy writing about faith more than politics. But I am convinced of this, the system will not keep itself honest. Nor will it be reformed from purely internal pressure.

To keep the stench bearable, there has to be some slice of the population willing to give up any advantages they could gain from participating in an establishment political party in order to work from the outside to make things better. Our system is pretty rotten right now, but I am convinced that it would be a whole lot worse were it not for people like us. And by "us", I no longer mean those who see things my way on most major policy issues. I mean those of us willing to take a journey on the outside.

THE END

Other Books by Mark Moore

Some of you may wonder exactly where I am on government. I've written two books on what amounts to "philosophy of government." They are...

Localism, a philosophy of government which ironically is less philosophical and more of a manifesto than...

Localism Defended, the Narrow Path Between Anarchy and the Central State

They are as relevant and needed now as they were on the day that I wrote them, the truth of this has only become more obvious.

I'll never write a more important book than Early Genesis: The Revealed Cosmology. It isn't an easy read and requires much thought and prayer, because (to our shame) the church is not accustomed to looking at these passages in the way that Christ said to look at them! If you care about the scriptures, and are up for a difficult read and can only read one more of my books, this is the one I'd want you to read.

I have also written a couple of fiction e-books- just fun-reading novellas. They are John Henry: Race Against the Robot in which the folk hero is alive in our time and a champion race car driver. He is about to retire when a giant tech company announces they have developed a driverless car that can beat any man alive. My other e-book is set in World War One, Thorns of the Rose. It is historical-fiction that weaves a story around people and events from World War One. In addition, I edited a little gift-book for my friend Dan Johnson, Senior Graduation.

Made in the USA
Columbia, SC
25 May 2021